THE REAL EASY BOOK
TUNES FOR BEGINNING IMPROVISERS

A Sher Music Co. Publication
Produced in conjunction with
the Stanford jazz Workshop
stanfordjazz.org

Expanded Arrangements and Music Engraving by Larry Dunlap

Original Conception and editing by - Michael Zisman
Educational Consultants - Bennett Paster, Ray Scott, James Nadel,
Mark Levine, Scott Sorkin and David Yamasaki
Original Music Engraving - Chuck Gee
Cover Design - Attila Nagy, Santa Rosa, CA and Ani Sher, Petaluma, CA

ISBN 1-883217-18-0

Index of Tunes

Introduction to the Expanded, 3-Horn Edition

Volume 1 of *The Real Easy Book* has proven to be one of the most popular publications from Sher Music Company. With its collection of relatively simple, but very important jazz compositions with accompanying educational material (Useful Scales, Sample Piano and Guitar voicings and Bass Lines), it has become one of the most valued resources for teachers of beginning jazz musicians.

Be assured, these same materials are included in this new Expanded Edition of the book. Musicians can still use the original version of Volume 1, if desired. However as you look at the charts in this updated version, you will see additional sections to each tune as well as second and third horn parts, making the tunes more interesting to play (see below).

The original versions included the single melody line of each tune with a facing page of the accompanying materials mentioned above. Educators have told us that a valuable addition would be harmony and background parts that could be played by other members of the ensemble.

So this Expanded, 3-Horn Edition adds supplemental harmony and background parts to be played by additional horns. We know that this additional material will be of great benefit to the many jazz combos using this book, allowing for fuller, richer, more varied performances of these classic tunes.

ADDITIONAL PARTS

You will now find 2nd and 3rd parts for each tune. These are parts that will harmonize with or accompany the melody of each tune (now called Part 1).

These additional parts are written to be easily played by beginning musicians. For the most part, they are kept within a limited range so as to be playable by as wide a variety of instruments as possible

With a few exceptions, any of the parts can be played by trumpet, trombone, any of the saxophones, guitar, flute (often one octave higher than written), or any other instrument.

In an ideal situation the parts would be distributed as follows:
- Part 1 would be played by trumpet, alto sax, flute or guitar.
- Part 2 is best for alto or tenor sax (often trombone as well).
- Part 3 is best for trombone, tenor sax or baritone sax.
But again, I stress that the parts were written to be playable by nearly any instrument.

ENDINGS

The melody of each tune is also known in jazz vernacular as the "head." In all cases in this book solos are played using the chords written over these melodies.

In this edition, specific ENDINGS are indicated for each tune. Occasionally this is a *Fine* ending within the tune. More often, a Coda has now been added which will serve as an ending after the "out chorus."

(continued on following page)

ADDED BACKGROUNDS, SHOUT CHORUSES

In this Expanded Edition, you also have additional sections added:
BACKGROUNDS to solos and/or SHOUT CHORUSES.
These are optional, but add form and interest to the tunes.

The Backgrounds can be played at any time to accompany any solo(s). Feel free to repeat them as desired.
They are written in two parts, in unison or harmony.

These Backgrounds may be played by Part 1 or Part 2 (identical to Part 1) together with Part 3 (a separate part). So these backgrounds are ideal behind solos by Part 1 or 2 or a rhythm section player.
(Generally Parts 1 and 2 in unison would sound fine as a background to a solo by Part 3.)

Shout Choruses have been added to many of the tunes.
They have three distinct parts and are to be played by Parts 1, 2 and 3 together.

These Shout Choruses could be played anytime after the initial "head" of the tune—before, between or after solos. However, they are generally meant to be played after all solos, before returning to the "out head."
They end with either a "D.C" or a "D.S.," and include any necessary pick-up notes.

IN CLOSING

The supplemental parts will add a lot of variety and interest to the performance of the tunes in Volume 1 of *The Real Easy Book*. They provide parts to be added to the melodies of the tunes, both harmonies/accompaniments and entirely new sections.

Remember that the Backgrounds and Shout Choruses can be inserted wherever you like in the performance of a tune.

Have a great time with these additions to one of our most popular publications!

Larry Dunlap, arranger

What is unique about this book?

The Real Easy Book was originally developed for the combo classes at the Stanford Jazz Workshop to provide a collection of jazz compositions that sounded good, were easy to learn and fun to play, and that were flexible enough to accommodate a variety of teaching approaches.

Written by well-known jazz artists, the compositions in *The Real Easy Book* are great examples of the jazz tunes, with characteristic melodies, phrasing, harmony, rhythm, and form. Since they were conceived as jazz tunes, they sound great on the first reading. This makes learning jazz more fun, and avoids the problem of making more advanced standards sound like jazz if you don't yet have the experience and interpretive skills required to do so.

By playing these tunes and mastering the techniques and elements they contain, you'll develop a jazz sensibility that you'll be able to apply to any music. Because of their rhythmic strength and phrasing, many of these compositions will sound good in other styles, such as Latin, funk, or rock.

The Real Easy Book is not intended to be a method book, but with its readable lead-sheets, flexible arrangements, concise improvisation elements, and rhythm section techniques, we hope that it will be helpful to any student, teacher, or band director.
- Individual students can study alone or use The Real Easy Book in conjunction with private instruction.
- Jazz teachers can use this book to teach their lessons for jazz students and combos.
- Band directors can use the tunes in The Real Easy Book as a starting point for developing performance ensembles.
- Band directors can adapt the arrangements for nearly any combination of instruments.

In all four transpositions of *The Real Easy Book*, each tune includes corresponding scales for improvisation, chord voicings, and bass lines. This makes it easier for educators to guide students as they apply new concepts to the requirements of particular compositions.

Please check out the Appendices for a detailed guide to chord types and their complementary scales, the Circle of Fifths, how to transpose, drum patterns, and discography of recordings of the tunes contained in *The Real Easy Book*.

Many of these great tunes are part of the common jazz repertoire, so students can play them at jam sessions, concerts, and gigs. We hope *The Real Easy Book* brings you many happy hours as you learn to master one of the greatest art forms ever created: jazz music!

Please Note

Unlike the tunes contained in other publications in Sher Music's *New Real Book* series, the lead sheets in *The Real Easy Book* are not transcriptions from recordings. Instead, the tunes contained here have been adapted or simplified from the original version so that students can more easily master the melodies and focus on the fundamentals of jazz. The definitive versions of many of these tunes can be found in several books in *The New Real Book* series, available at www.shermusic.com.

How to use this book

The Songs: Each tune is presented as a lead-sheet with the melody, as well as with full arrangements for two additional harmonized instrumental parts, plus shout chorus and endings. This makes it easy to have full-sounding performances with a wide variety of possible instrumentation.

On some songs, the chords have been simplified to make the harmonic movement clear. In all cases, chords appear over the beats on which they should be played. When no additional chord symbols appear, the current chord should continue to be played, even over multiple bars. Some songs have short forms, such as 8-bar forms and 12-bar blues forms. On these tunes, you can repeat the melody before and after each solo.

The Supplemental Material: Chord voicings, scales for improvisation, and suggested bass lines are provided for each tune to help students apply concepts of jazz performance to the particular needs of each song. *The Real Easy Book* is not a method book, however, and there are many books that provide excellent instruction on all kinds of jazz topics, such as *The Jazz Theory Book* by Mark Levine and *The Blues Scales* by Dan Greenblatt, both available at www.shermusic.com.

The Numbers: The Arabic numbers you see under or next to notes in the Supplemental Material refer to the scale degree represented by each note, in relation to the root of the current chord. Since each scale has just 7 notes, note that scale degrees 2 and 9 refer to the same note name, as do 4 and 11, and also 6 and 13.

The Piano Voicings: For each tune, two sets of piano chord voicings are provided for comping. The Basic 3-Note Voicings illustrate the root motion and resolution of 3rds and 7ths through the chord progression. Students should start with these voicings in order to understand the voice-leading of each tune. As with standard piano music, play the treble staff in your right hand and the bass staff in your left. Invert the 3rds and 7ths to create an additional set of voicings, and to change the register the voicings occupy.

The Rootless Voicings do not include chord roots. These voicings are more typical of those used by professional jazz pianists, and it leaves the root to be played by the bass player. These voicings contain the 3rd, 7th, and one additional note of the corresponding chord. Play them in either hand, divide the notes up between your hands, and transpose them when supporting different soloists. The voice-leading is smooth, making hand motion efficient. Pianists should use these voicings when comping during their own improvisations.

In some cases, the voicings contain notes not reflected in the corresponding chord symbols. It's common practice for jazz pianists to add the 9th, 11th, and 13th of a chord as needed, even when not spelled out in the chord symbol. Where appropriate, these upper extension notes have been added to the voicings.

The Scales: One common and useful approach to improvisation is to base your solo on particular scales. The Useful Scales section of each tune provides one or more scales that relate to the harmony of the song, along with the corresponding chords. These are suggestions for students to use as they begin their exploration of improvisation. In most cases there are may be additional scale possibilities that students can learn about with the guidance of a teacher or with a jazz method book.

The Bass Lines: For each tune, one chorus of a sample bass line is provided to give the student an initial idea of how to create an appropriate bass part. Analyze the note choices and rhythms, and create your own bass lines. If the musical style is changed, for example from swing to bossa nova, note that the bass line indicated my no longer be appropriate for the style.

The Guitar Voicings: Several possible fingerings are provided for many of the chord voicings in this book. These voicings are interchangeable, and guitarists and pianists should listen carefully to each other and change the register of their chord voicings to avoid clashing.

The Drum Parts: Basic drum patters for several styles are included in Appendix 1. Most songs in The Real Easy Book sound good with these patterns, as well as with patterns the student may already know.

Study Hints:
- Memorize the melody, chords, voicings, scales, and patterns for each tune that you work on. By internalizing these elements, you'll be able to use them more freely as you improvise.
- Look for connections and common elements between songs, such as scale and chord relationships, form, and harmonic movement. Finding similarities make learning additional songs easier.
- Use the Supplemental Material as a starting point as you improvise. Experiment with additional scales, patterns, and ideas. Ask your teachers and other musicians for suggestions of other elements to apply to improvising on tunes you know.
- Using the discography in Appendix II, search for the original recordings of the tunes you're working on and listen to them to see how other musicians play them.
- Apply your own creativity and imagination as much as possible. Play songs you know in different styles. Use the arrangements and endings provided here as springboards for your own arrangements.

Some Important Definitions

Form: Song forms that have multiple sections are usually delineated with letters. "Killer Joe," for example, has two sections, A and B. The A section is played twice (A1 and A2), then the B section (also called the Bridge), followed by a restatement of the A section (A3). This is called the AABA form. Other song forms you'll find in The Real Easy Book include ABA, AAB, and ABAC. Another common song form you'll find in this book is the 12-bar blues; in this case, "blues" indicates only the form, and is not meant to imply a particular style.

Rhythmic Feels: All the songs in The Real Easy Book will sound good played with different rhythmic feels, but on each tune, we've indicated the feel used on the original recordings.
- Swing: In swing, any two consecutive eighth notes during one beat are played as an eighth-note triplet figure, with the first two notes tied together, rather than as eighth notes of equal value.
- Jazz Waltz: This applies the same feel as swing, but in 3/4 meter.
- Straight-Eighth: Used with Latin, rock, and funk styles, this style sounds best when eighth notes are played evenly.

Tempo: In most cases, we've indicated the general tempo at which each song was originally played. Here are the equivalents in beats per minute (bpm):
- Slow: quarter note = 80-120 bpm
- Medium: quarter note = 120-180 bpm
- Fast: quarter note = 180 bpm and above

About the Stanford Jazz Workshop

The Stanford Jazz Workshop (SJW) provides innovative jazz education programs for all musicians. Since its founding in 1972 by Jim Nadel, SJW has brought the top artists in jazz together with students of all ages, backgrounds, and abilities to join in an immersive learning environment that fosters close communication and idea sharing. The list of musicians who have been on the SJW faculty is a veritable Who's Who of jazz, and includes such late, great artists as Stan Getz, Dizzy Gillespie, McCoy Tyner, Horace Silver, Ray Brown, James Moody, Charlie Haden, and Joe Henderson, as well as leading contemporary performers such as Chick Corea, Joe Lovano, Fred Hersch, Branford Marsalis, Regina Carter, the Bad Plus, Bill Frisell, and many more. Many of the thousands of SJW students and alumni over the years have become leading jazz artists themselves, such as Julian Lage, Joshua Redman, Taylor Eigsti, Larry Grenadier, Ambrose Akinmusire, Ethan Iverson, Bill Stewart, Sylvia Cuenca, Mark Turner, and Dayna Stephens.

Emphasizing improvisation, ear training, technique, and individual creativity, the SJW curriculum is tailored to meet the needs of instrumentalists and vocalists at every stage of development. SJW offers week-long summer camps at Stanford University as well as year-round courses and ensembles at a variety of locations, with programs for middle school students, high school students, college students, adult amateurs, jazz educators, and professional musicians. SJW's summer programs are integrated with the renowned Stanford Jazz Festival, which presents some of the best jazz artists performing today. Many of the artists presented at the Stanford Jazz Festival are on the faculty of SJW's Jazz Camp and Jazz Institute summer immersion programs, so students can study with master musicians during the day, see them perform at night, and hang out with them at jam sessions. This is just one of the many elements of SJW that make its jazz education programs among the best in the world.

SJW is excited to partner with Sher Music to provide this expanded version of *The Real Easy Book*. Special thanks to Chuck Sher for his support of the entire *Real Easy Book* series, to Larry Dunlap for the fantastic arrangements in this edition, and to Scott Sorkin and Dave Yamasaki for updating the guitar chord diagrams. *The Real Easy Book* series has been developed and refined over many years of use at SJW's summer immersion programs, with major contributions from jazz artists such as Michael Zisman, Bennett Paster, Ray Scott, Mark Levine, Bert Carelli, Carma Burglund, Alex Kharmats, Gregory Ryan, John McKenna, Bob Parlocha, Matt Clark, Brad Buethe, Larry Dunlap, Dena DeRose, Andrew Speight, the late, great Chuck Gee, and many more, as well as from hundreds if not thousands of SJW students. Extra special thanks to Jim Nadel for his vision and leadership for over 40 years at the Stanford Jazz Workshop.

Find out more about all of the Stanford Jazz Workshop programs at stanfordjazz.org.

The Tunes

RAY BROWN, OSCAR PETERSON & HERB ELLIS
Photo©Paul Hoeffler, Toronto, Canada

Bags' Groove (Part 1 - melody)

Milt Jackson

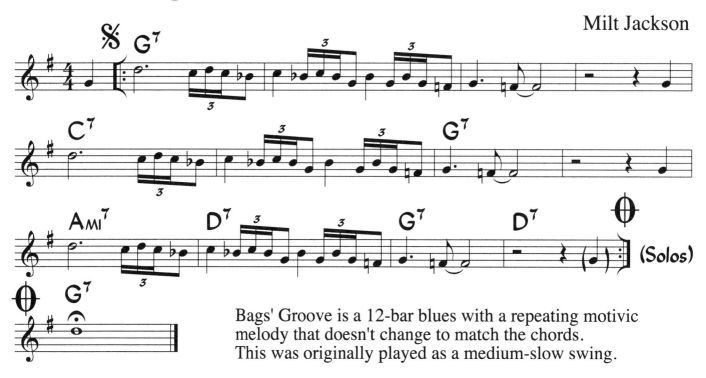

Bags' Groove is a 12-bar blues with a repeating motivic melody that doesn't change to match the chords.
This was originally played as a medium-slow swing.

On Cue: Background for solos. (Duplicates Part 2). All can play as written.

Shout chorus (3 parts). Play after solos (optional). All can play as written.

D.S. al Coda

Supplemental Material - Bags' Groove

Sample Piano Voicings

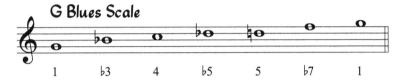

Useful Scales

Sample Bass Line

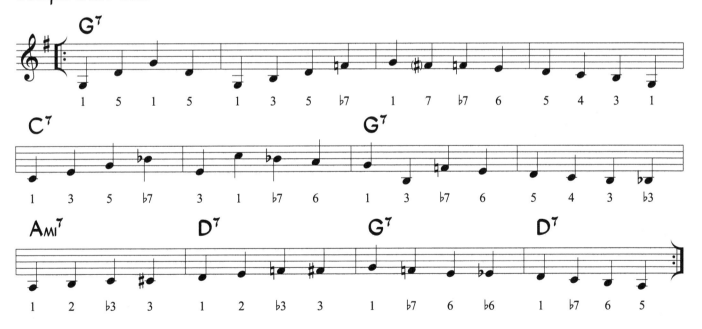

4

Bags' Groove (Part 2 - harmony)

Tenor play upper octave. Others play lower octave.

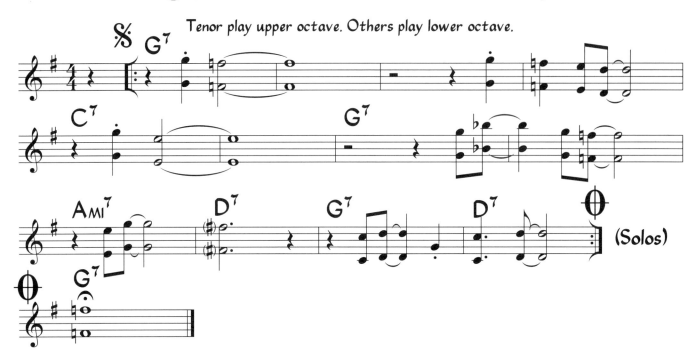

On Cue: Background for solos. All can play as written.

Shout chorus . Play after solos (optional). Tenor play upper octave. Others play lower octave.

Useful scales: G Blues Scale

1   b3   4   b5   5   b7   1

Bags' Groove (Part 3 - harmony)

Tenor play upper octave. Others play lower octave.

(Solos)

On Cue: Background for solos. All can play as written.

Shout chorus. Play after solos (optional). Tenor play upper octave. Others play lower octave.

D.S. al Coda

Useful scales: G Blues Scale

1   b3   4   b5   5   b7   1

Big Bertha (Part 1 - melody)

Duke Pearson

Big Bertha has an ABBA form. The rests in the A section melody leave spaces for the rhythm section (or the added horns) to fill. This was originally played with a medium swing feel.

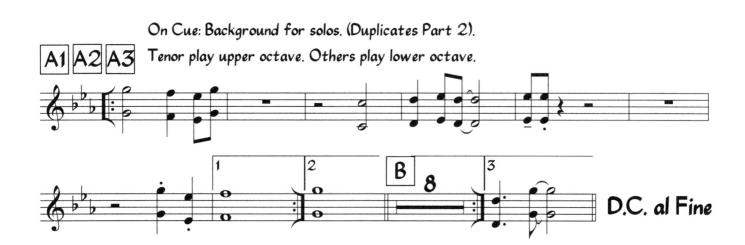

Supplemental Material - Big Bertha

Sample Piano Voicings

Basic 3-note voicings   Rootless voicings

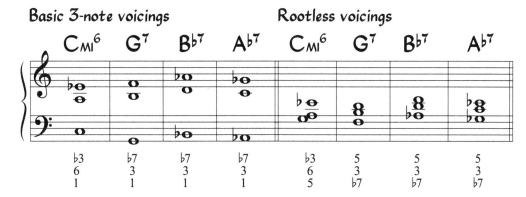

Useful Scales

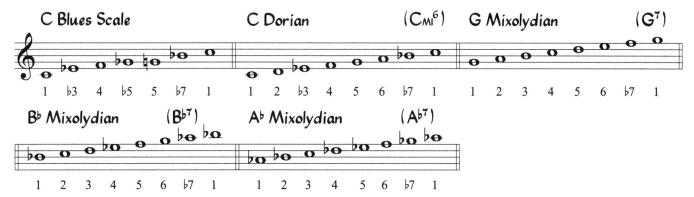

Sample Bass Line

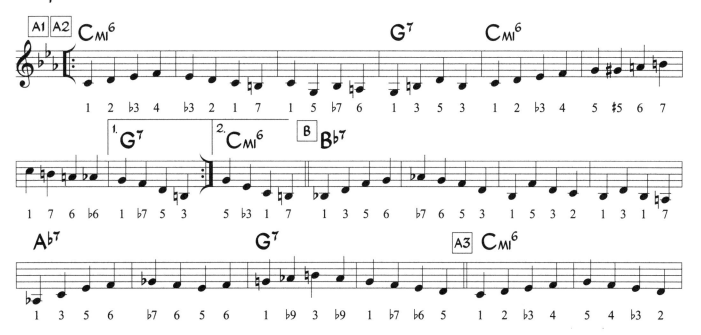

Big Bertha (Part 2 - harmony)

Big Bertha (Part 3 - harmony)

Blue Seven (Part 1 - melody)

Sonny Rollins

Blue Seven is a 12-bar blues that features a call and response melody. Note the use of the b5 (also called the #11) in the melody over each of the three seventh chords. This was originally played as a medium-slow swing.

On Cue: Background for solos. All can play this part as written.

Shout chorus. Play after solos (optional). Tenor play upper octave. Others play lower octave.

D.C. al Coda

Supplemental Material - Blue Seven

Sample Piano Voicings

Basic 3-note voicings   Rootless voicings

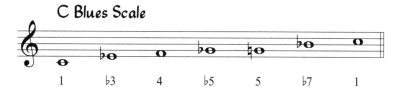

	3	♭7	♭7	9	13	5
	♭7	3	3	♭7	3	3
	1	1	1	3	♭7	♭7

Useful Scales

C Blues Scale

| 1 | ♭3 | 4 | ♭5 | 5 | ♭7 | 1 |

Sample Bass Line

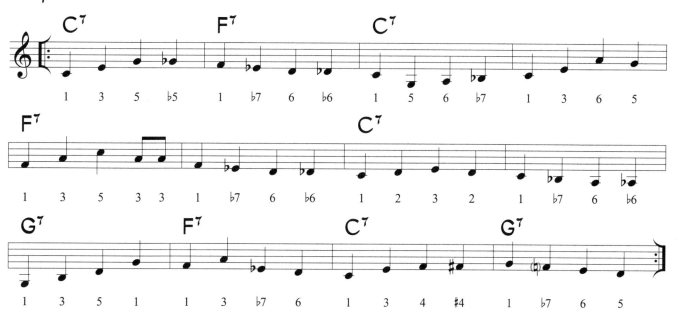

Blue Seven (Part 2 - harmony)

Tenor play upper octave. Others play lower octave.

On Cue: Background for solos. All can play this part as written.

Shout chorus. Play after solos (optional). Tenor play upper octave. Others play lower octave.

D.C. al Coda

Useful scales: C Blues Scale

1   b3   4   b5   5   b7   1

Blue Seven (Part 3 - harmony)

Tenor play upper octave. Others play lower octave.

On Cue: Background for solos. All can play this part as written.

Shout chorus. Play after solos (optional). Tenor play upper octave. Others play lower octave.

D.C. al Coda

Useful scales: C Blues Scale

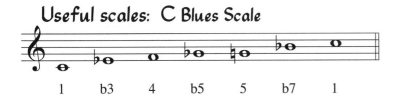

1   b3   4   b5   5   b7   1

Blues by Five (Part 1 - melody)

Red Garland

Blues By Five is a 12-bar blues where sections of the motivic melody are transposed to match the chord changes. This was originally played with a medium-swing feel.

On Cue: Background for solos. (Duplicates Part 2). Tenor play upper octave. Others play lower octave.

Shout chorus (3 parts). Play after solos (optional). All play single notes as written.

For octaves: Tenor play upper note, others play lower note.

D.S. al Fine

Supplemental Material - Blues By Five

Sample Piano Voicings

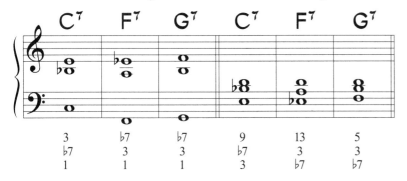

Useful Scales

Sample Bass Line

16

Blues by Five (Part 2 - harmony)

Tenor play upper octave. Others play lower octave.

On Cue: Background for solos. Tenor play upper octave. Others play lower octave.

Shout chorus. Play after solos (optional). All play single notes as written.

For octaves: Tenor play upper note. Others play lower note.

D.S. al Fine

Useful scales: C Blues Scale

Blues by Five (Part 3 - harmony)

All play single notes as written.
For octaves: Tenor play upper note. Others play lower note.

On Cue: Background for solos. Tenor play upper octave. Others play lower octave.

Shout chorus. Play after solos (optional). All play single notes as written.

For octaves: Tenor play upper note. Others play lower note.

D.S. al Fine

Useful scales: C Blues Scale

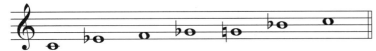

Blues in the Closet (Part 1 - melody)

Oscar Pettiford

Blues In The Closet is a 12-bar blues with a motivic melody.
One melody note gets changed in measure 5 so that the melody
matches the chord changes. This was originally played with a medium-slow swing feel.

On Cue: Background for solos. (Duplicates Part 2) Tenor play upper octave. Others play lower octave.

Shout chorus (3 parts). Play after solos (optional). All can play as written.

Supplemental Material - Blues In The Closet

Sample Piano Voicings

Useful Scales

Sample Bass Line

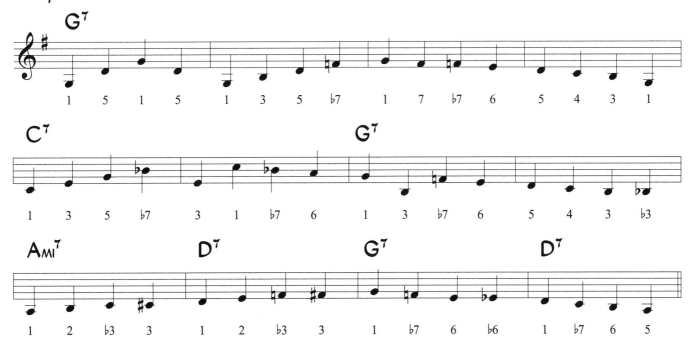

20

Blues in the Closet (Part 2 - harmony)

On Cue: Background for solos. Tenor play upper octave. Others play lower octave.

Shout chorus (3 parts). Play after solos (optional). All play single notes as written.

For octaves: Tenor play upper note, others play lower note.

D.S. al Coda

Useful scales: G Blues Scale

Blues in the Closet (Part 3 - harmony)

All play single lines. For octs.: Tenor play upper notes, others play lower notes.

(Solos)

On Cue: Background for solos. Tenor play upper octave. Others play lower octave.

Shout chorus (3 parts). Play after solos (optional). All play single notes as written.

For octaves: Tenor play upper note, others play lower note.

D.S. al Coda

Useful scales: G Blues Scale

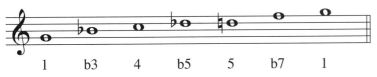

1   b3   4   b5   5   b7   1

Cold Duck Time (Part 1 - melody)

Eddie Harris

Cold Duck Time has a 12-bar form, but it does not use the typical 12-bar blues chord progression. It was originally played with a straight-eighth feel.

On Cue: Background for solos. (Duplicates Part 2) Tenor play upper octave. Others play lower octave.

Shout chorus (3 parts). Play after solos (optional). All play single notes as written.

For octaves: Tenor play upper note, others play lower note.

Supplemental Material - Cold Duck Time

Sample Piano Voicings

Basic 3-note voicings   Rootless voicings

Useful Scales

Sample Bass Line

Cold Duck Time (Part 2 - harmony)

Useful scales: G Blues Scale   Eb Major (E♭MA7)   F Major (FMA7)

Cold Duck Time (Part 3 - harmony)

Tenor play upper octave. Others play lower octave.

(Solos)

On Cue: Background for solos. Tenor play upper octave. Others play lower octave.

Shout chorus (3 parts). Play after solos (optional). All play single notes as written.

For octaves: Tenor play upper note, others play lower note.

D.S. al Coda

Useful scales: G Blues Scale   Eb Major (EᵇMA⁷)   F Major (FMA⁷)

1 b3 4 b5 5 b7 1   1 2 3 4 5 6 7 1   1 2 3 4 5 6 7 1

Contemplation (Part 1 - melody)

McCoy Tyner

Comtemplation has a 16-bar form. The melodic phrases each end differently to match the chord changes. It was originally played with a slow jazz-waltz feel.

On Cue: Background for solos. (Duplicates Part 2) Tenor play upper octave. Others play lower octave.

Shout chorus (3 parts). Play after solos (optional). All play single notes as written.

For octaves: Tenor play upper note, others play lower note.

D.C. al Coda

Supplemental Material - Contemplation

Sample Piano Voicings

Basic 3-note voicings   Rootless voicings

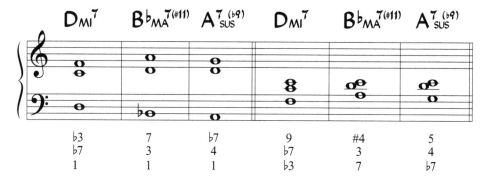

Useful Scales

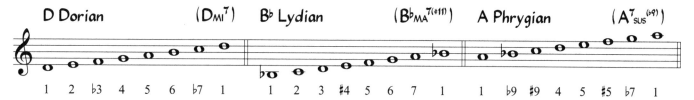

Sample Bass Line

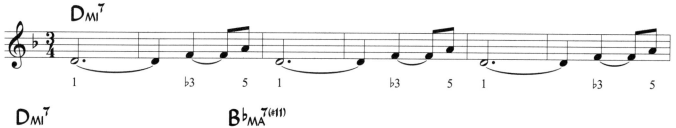

28

Contemplation (Part 2 - harmony)

Contemplation (Part 3 - harmony)

Doxy (Part 1 - melody)

Sonny Rollins

Doxy has a 16-bar form. It was originally played with a medium-slow swing feel.

On Cue: Background for solos. (Duplicates Part 2)

Tenor play upper octave. Others play lower octave.

Supplemental Material - Doxy

Sample Piano Voicings

Basic 3-note voicings

Rootless voicings

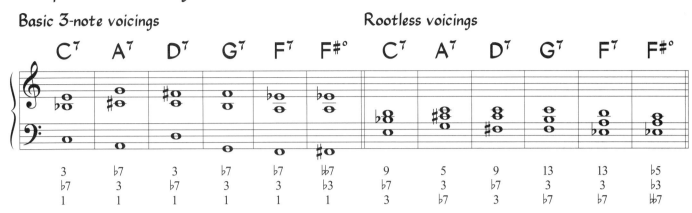

Useful Scales

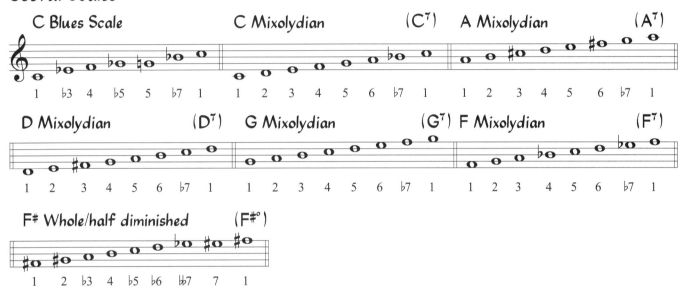

Sample Bass Line

Doxy (Part 2 - harmony)

All play single lines. For octaves: Tenor play upper note, others play lower note.

On Cue: Background for solos. Tenor play upper octave. Others play lower octave.

(for D.S.)

(after solos)
D.S. al Coda

Useful scales:

Doxy (Part 3 - harmony)

All play single lines. For octaves: Tenor play upper note, others play lower note.

On Cue: Background for solos. All play single lines. For octs: Tenor play upper note. Others play lower note.

(for D.S.)

(after solos)
D.S. al Coda

Useful scales:

Edward Lee (Part 1 - melody)

Harold Mabern

Edward Lee was originally played with a medium-swing feel.

On Cue: Background for solos. (Duplicates Part 2)
Tenor play upper notes. Others play lower notes.

(after last solo)

D.C. al Coda

Supplemental Material - Edward Lee

Sample Piano Voicings

Basic 3-note voicings

Rootless voicings

Useful Scales

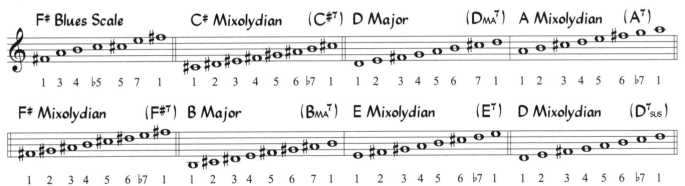

Sample Bass Line

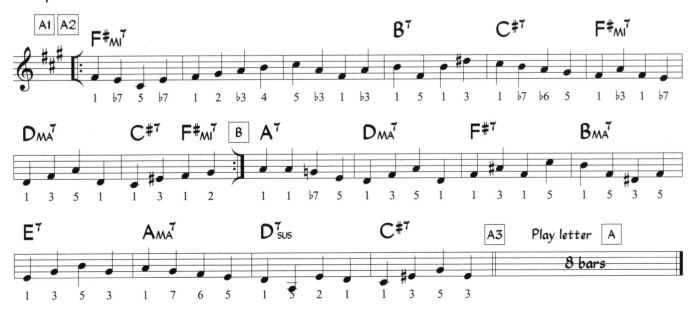

Edward Lee (Part 2 - harmony)

Edward Lee (Part 3 - harmony)

Equinox (Part 1 - melody)

John Coltrane

Equinox is a 12-bar minor blues. It was originally played with a slow swing feel.

On Cue: Background for solos. (Duplicates Part 2) Tenor play upper octave. Others play lower octave.

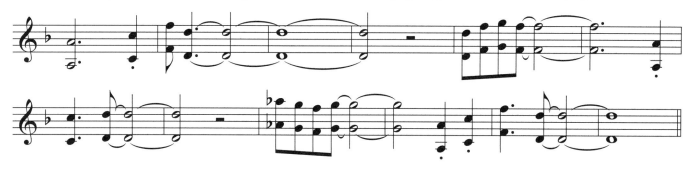

Shout chorus (3 parts). Play after solos (optional). All play as written.

D.S. al Coda

Supplemental Material - Equinox

Sample Piano Voicings

Useful Scales

Sample Bass Lines

Equinox (Part 2 - harmony)

Equinox (Part 3 - harmony)

Useful scales:

Freedom Jazz Dance

Eddie Harris

Freedom Jazz Dance was originally played with a straight-eighth feel.

On Cue: Background for solos. (Duplicates Part 2).
Tenor play upper octave. Others play lower octave.

Shout chorus (3 parts). Play after solos (optional). All play single lines.
For octaves; Tenor play upper notes. Others play lower notes..

Supplemental Material - Freedom Jazz Dance

Sample Piano Voicings

Basic 3-note voicings   Rootless voicings

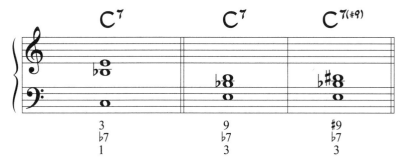

Useful Scales

C Blues Scale

Sample Bass Line

44

Freedom Jazz Dance (Part 2 - harmony)

Tenor play upper octave. Others play lower octave.

(Fine)

On Cue: Background for solos. Tenor play upper octave. Others play lower octave.

Shout chorus. Play after solos (optional). All play single notes as written.

For octaves: Tenor play upper note. Others play lower note.

D.S. al Fine

Useful scales: C Blues Scale

1   b3   4   b5   5   b7   1

Freedom Jazz Dance (Part 3 - harmony)

Tenor play upper octave. Others play lower octave.

(Fine)

On Cue: Background for solos. All play single lines.

For octaves: Tenor play upper notes. Others play lower notes.

Shout chorus . Play after solos (optional). All play single lines.

For octaves: Tenor play upper notes. Others play lower notes.

D.S. al Fine

Useful scales: C Blues Scale

1   b3   4   b5   5   b7   1

Gingerbread Boy (Part 1 - melody)

Jimmy Heath

Tenor play upper octave. Others play lower octave.

Gingerbread Boy is a 16-bar modified blues. Solos are over a standard 12-bar blues progression. It was originally played with a medium swing.

(solo changes - 12-bar blues) Written notes are On Cue Background for solos.

Shout chorus . Play after solos (optional). Tenor play upper octave. Others play lower octave.

D.S. al Fine

Supplemental Material - Gingerbread Boy

Sample Piano Voicings

Basic 3 and 4-note voicings   Rootless voicings

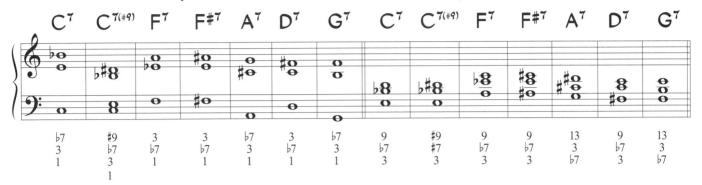

Useful Scales

Sample Bass Line

Gingerbread Boy (Part 2 - harmony)

Tenor play upper octave. Others play lower octave.

(solo changes - 12-bar blues) Written notes are On Cue Background for solos.

Shout chorus . Play after solos (optional). Tenor play upper octave. Others play lower octave.

Useful scales: C Blues Scale

Gingerbread Boy (Part 3 - harmony)

Tenor play upper octave. Others play lower octave.

(for D.S.)

(Fine)

(solo changes - 12-bar blues) Written notes are On Cue Background for solos.

Shout chorus . Play after solos (optional). Tenor play upper octave. Others play lower octave.

D.S. al Fine

Useful scales: C Blues Scale

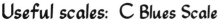

1   b3   4   b5   5   b7   1

Groove Merchant (Part 1 - melody)

Jerome Richardson

Groove Merchant was originally played with a medium-swing feel.

On Cue: Background for solos. (Duplicates Part 2) Tenor play upper octave. Others play lower octave.

Shout chorus Play after solos (optional). All play single notes as written.

For octaves: Tenor play upper note, others play lower note.

D.S. al Fine

(for D.S.)

Supplemental Material - Groove Merchant

Sample Piano Voicings

Basic 3-note voicings

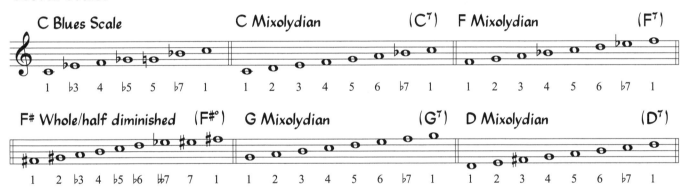

Rootless voicings

Useful scales

Sample Bass Line

52

Groove Merchant (Part 2 - harmony)

Tenor play upper notes, others play lower notes.

On Cue: Background for solos. Tenor play upper octave. Others play lower octave.

Shout chorus Play after solos (optional). All play single notes as written.

For octaves: Tenor play upper note, others play lower note.

D.S. al Fine

Useful scales: C Blues Scale

C Mixolydian (C⁷)

F Mixolydian (F⁷)

| 1 | b3 | 4 | b5 | 5 | b7 | 1 | | 1 | 2 | 3 | 4 | 5 | 6 | b7 | 1 | | 1 | 2 | 3 | 4 | 5 | 6 | b7 | 1 |

F# whole/half dimin. (F#°⁷)

G Mixolydian (G⁷)

D Mixolydian (D⁷)

| 1 | 2 | b3 | 4 | b5 | b6 | #6 | #7 | 1 | | 1 | 2 | 3 | 4 | 5 | 6 | b7 | 1 | | 1 | 2 | 3 | 4 | 5 | 6 | b7 | 1 |

Groove Merchant (Part 3 - harmony)

All play single lines. For octaves: Tenor play upper note, others play lower note.

On Cue: Background for solos. All play single lines. For octs: Tenor play upper note. Others play lower note.

Shout chorus Play after solos (optional). All play single notes as written.

For octaves: Tenor play upper note, others play lower note.

D.S. al Fine

Useful scales: C Blues Scale   C Mixolydian   (C⁷)   F Mixolydian (F⁷)

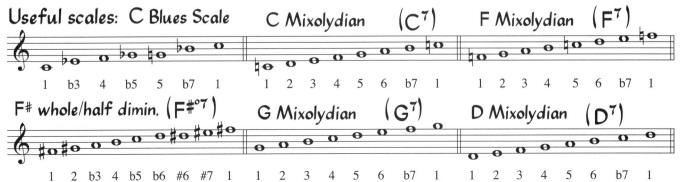

Jive Samba (Part 1 - melody)

Nat Adderley

Jive Samba was originally played with a straight-eighth feel.

On Cue: Background for solos. (Duplicates Part 2) All play single lines.
For octaves; Tenor play upper notes. Others play lower notes.

Supplemental Material - Jive Samba

Sample Piano Voicings

Basic 3-note voicings   Rootless voicings

Useful Scales

Sample Bass Line For Solos

56

Jive Samba (Part 2 - harmony)

All play single notes. For octaves: Tenor play upper note, others play lower note.

On Cue: Background for solos. (Duplicates Part 2) All play single lines.

For octaves; Tenor play upper notes. Others play lower notes.

D.S. al Coda

Useful scales: G Blues Scale

Jive Samba (Part 3 - harmony)

All play single notes. For octaves: Tenor play upper note, others play lower note.

On Cue: Background for solos. All play single lines.
For octaves: Tenor play upper notes. Others play lower notes.

Useful scales: G Blues Scale

Jo Jo Calypso (Part 1 - melody)

Jim Nadel

Jo Jo Calypso was originally played with a straight-eighth feel.

On Cue: Background for solos. (Duplicates Part 2) All play single lines.

For octs.: Tenor play upper notes. Others play lower notes.

Shout chorus. Play after solos (optional). All play this part.

(for D.S.)

D.S. al Coda

Supplemental Material - Jo Jo Calypso

Sample Piano Voicings

Basic 3-note voicings   Rootless voicings

G	A_{MI}⁷	D⁷	G	A_{MI}⁷	D⁷

3	♭3	♭7	5	5	9
5	♭7	3	3	♭3	♭7
1	1	1	6	♭7	3

Useful Scales

G Major Pentatonic (G)   A Dorian   (A_{MI}⁷)   D Mixolydian   (D⁷)

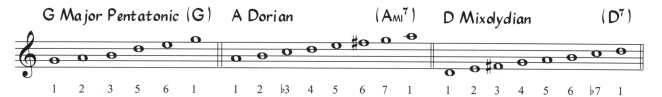

| 1 | 2 | 3 | 5 | 6 | 1 | | 1 | 2 | ♭3 | 4 | 5 | 6 | 7 | 1 | | 1 | 2 | 3 | 4 | 5 | 6 | ♭7 | 1 |

Sample Bass Line

G   A_{MI}⁷   D⁷   G   (etc.)

| 1 | 3 | 5 | 1 | 5 | ♭3 | 1 | 5 | 1 | 1 | 3 | 5 |

Jo Jo Calypso (Part 2 - harmony)

Tenor play upper notes, others play lower notes.

(Solos)

On Cue: Background for solos. All play single lines. For octs: Tenor play upper note. Others play lower note.

Shout chorus . Play after solos (optional). Tenor play upper notes. Others play lower notes.

D.S. al Coda

Useful scales:
G Major Pentatonic (G)   A Dorian (Ami⁷)   D Mixolydian (D⁷)

Jo Jo Calypso (Part 3 - harmony)

The Jody Grind (Part 1 - melody)

Horace Silver

The Jody Grind is a 12-bar blues with unusual harmony on the turnaround (the last 4 bars). It was originally played with a straight-eighth feel.

On Cue: Background for solos. (Duplicates Part 2) Tenor play upper octave. Others play lower octave.

Shout chorus Play after solos (optional). All play single notes as written.

For octaves: Tenor play upper note, others play lower note.

D.S. al Fine

Supplemental Material - The Jody Grind

Sample Piano Voicings

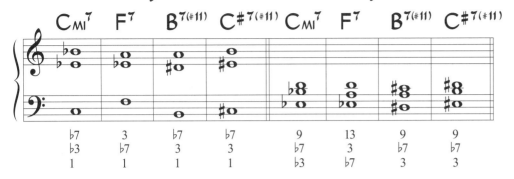

Useful Scales

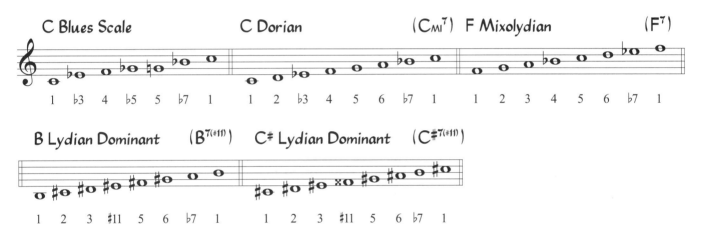

Sample Bass Line

The Jody Grind (Part 2 - harmony)

The Jody Grind (Part 3 - harmony)

All play single lines. For octaves: Tenor play upper note, others play lower note.

On Cue: Background for solos. Tenor play upper octave. Others play lower octave.

Shout chorus Play after solos (optional). All play single notes as written.

For octaves: Tenor play upper note, others play lower note.

Killer Joe (Part 1 - melody)

Benny Golson

Killer Joe has a 32-bar AABA form. The extreme contrast between the A and B sections creates a great sense of tension and release. It was originally played with a medium-swing feel.

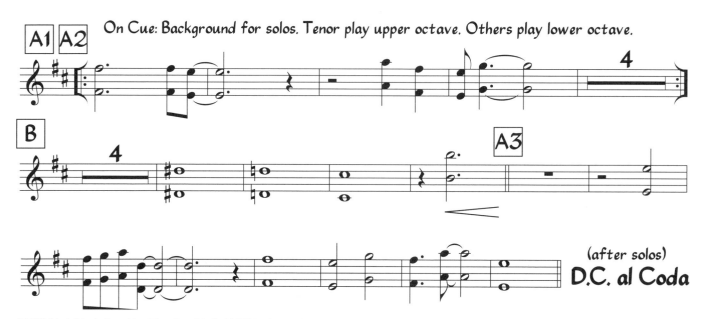

Supplemental Material - Killer Joe

Sample Piano Voicings

Basic 3-note voicings

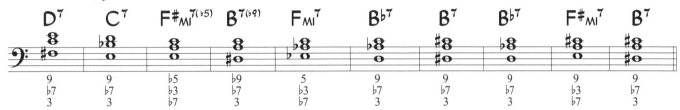

Rootless voicings

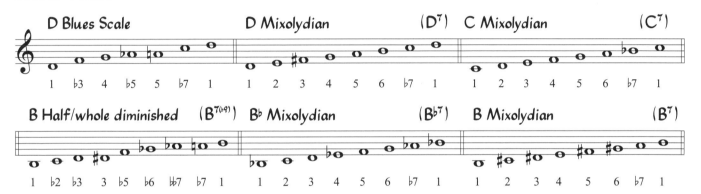

Useful Scales

Sample Bass Line

Killer Joe (Part 2 - harmony)

Killer Joe (Part 3 - harmony)

Listen Here (Part 1 - melody)

Eddie Harris

All play single notes as written. For octs. Tenor play upper note. Others play lower note.

Listen Here was originally played with a straight-eighth feel.
This chart is based on an arrangement by AJ Nadel.

On Cue: Background for solos. (Duplicates Part 2)

Supplemental Material - Listen Here

Sample Piano Voicings

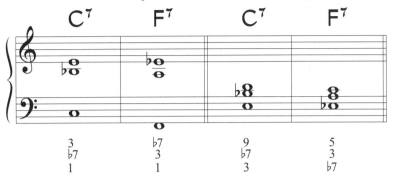

Useful Scales

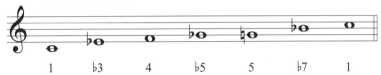

Sample Piano & Bass

Listen Here (Part 2 - harmony)

All play single notes as written. For octs. Tenor play upper note. Others play lower note.
(1st x: horns: 2 & 3 only, no rhythm section)

Listen Here (Part 3 - harmony)

All play single notes as written. For octs. Tenor play upper note. Others play lower note.
(1st x: horns: 2 & 3 only, no rhythm section)

Useful scales: C Blues Scale

Little Sunflower (Part 1 - melody)

Freddie Hubbard

Little Sunflower was originally played with a straight-eighth feel.

Supplemental Material - Little Sunflower

Sample Piano Voicings

Basic 3-note voicings   Rootless voicings

b3	3	3	9	9	9
b7	7	7	b7	7	7
1	1	1	b3	3	3

Useful Scales

E Dorian (Emi7): 1 2 b3 4 5 6 b7 1
F Lydian (Fma7): 1 2 3 #4 5 6 7 1
E Major (Ema7): 1 2 3 4 5 6 7 1

Sample Bass Line

Little Sunflower (Part 2 - harmony)

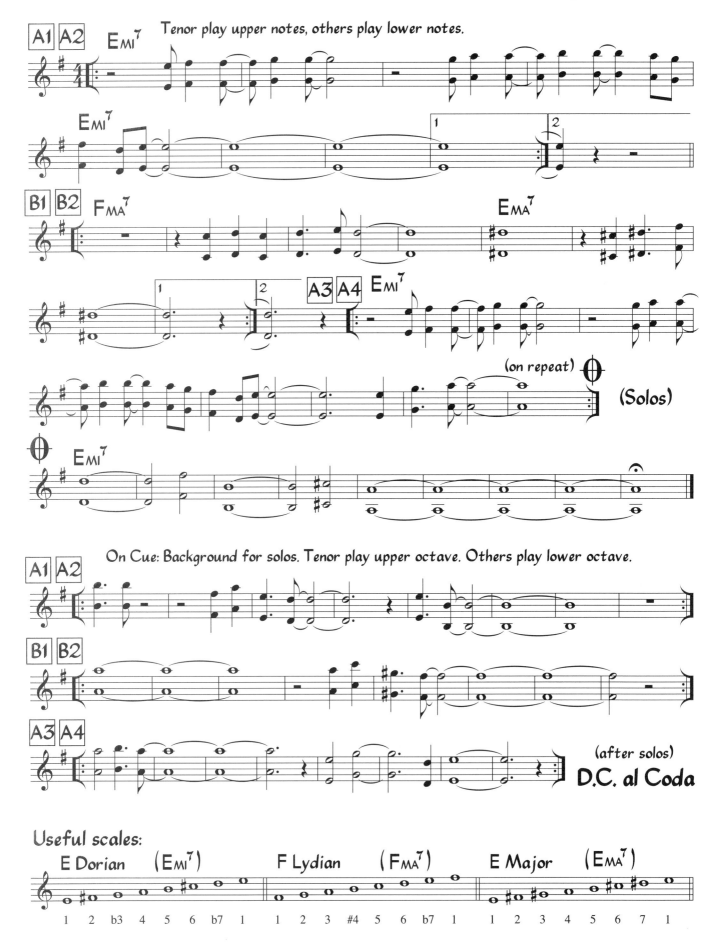

Little Sunflower (Part 3 - harmony)

Mercy, Mercy, Mercy (Part 1 - melody)

Joe Zawinul

All play single lines. For octaves: Tenor play upper note, Others play lower note.

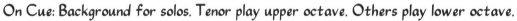

(Solos)

Mercy, Mercy, Mercy was originally played with a slow straight-eighth feel.

On Cue: Background for solos. Tenor play upper octave. Others play lower octave.

(after solos)
D.C. al Coda

Supplemental Material - Mercy, Mercy, Mercy

Sample Piano Voicings

Basic 3-note voicings

Root and rootless voicings

Useful Scales

Sample Bass Line

Mercy, Mercy, Mercy (Part 2 - harmony)

Mercy, Mercy, Mercy (Part 3 - harmony)

All play single lines. For octaves: Tenor play upper note, Others play lower note.

On Cue: Background for solos. All play single lines. For octs: Tenor play upper note, others play lower note.

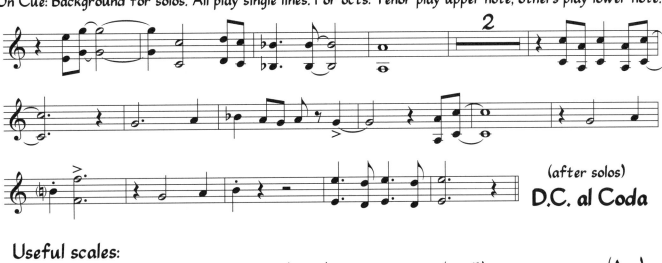

(after solos)
D.C. al Coda

Useful scales:
C Blues Scale   D Dorian (Dмi⁷)   E Dorian (Eмi⁷)   A Aeolian (Aмi)

1 b3 4 b5 5 b7 1   1 2 b3 4 5 6 b7 1   1 2 b3 4 5 6 b7 1   1 2 b3 4 5 b6 b7 1

Midnight Waltz (Part 1 - melody)

Cedar Walton

Midnight Waltz is a 24-bar blues that explores the tension and resolution between suspended 7th and dominant 7th chords. The C7sus and F7sus chords can all be played as straight dominant 7th chords for the solos. This song was originally played with a jazz-waltz feel.

Shout chorus. Play after solos (optional). All play single notes as written.

For octaves: Tenor play upper note, others play lower note.

©1992 Vernita Music Co. Used by Permission

Supplemental Material - Midnight Waltz

Sample Piano Voicings

Basic 3-note voicings   Rootless voicings

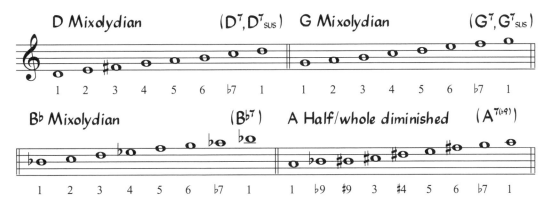

Useful Scales

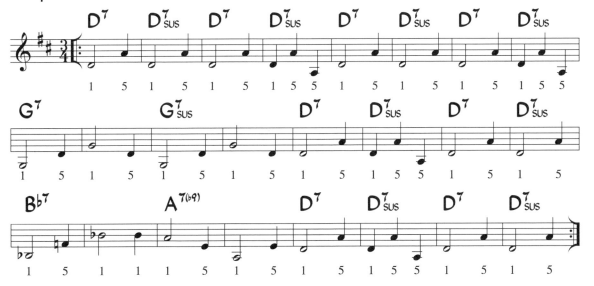

Sample Bass Line

Midnight Waltz (Part 2 - harmony)

Tenor play upper octave. Others play lower octave.

(Solos)

Shout chorus. Play after solos (optional). All play single notes as written.

For octaves: Tenor play upper note, others play lower note.

D.S. al Coda

Useful scales:

D Mixolydian (D⁷, D⁷ₛᵤₛ) G Mixolydian (G⁷, G⁷ₛᵤₛ) Bb Mixolydian (Bb⁷) A half/whole dimin. (A⁷⁽ᵇ⁹⁾)

1 2 3 4 5 6 b7 1   1 2 3 4 5 6 b7 1   1 2 3 4 5 6 b7 1   1 b2 b3 3 b5 5 6 b7 1

86

Mr. P.C. (Part 1 - melody)

Tenor play upper octave. Others play lower octave.

John Coltrane

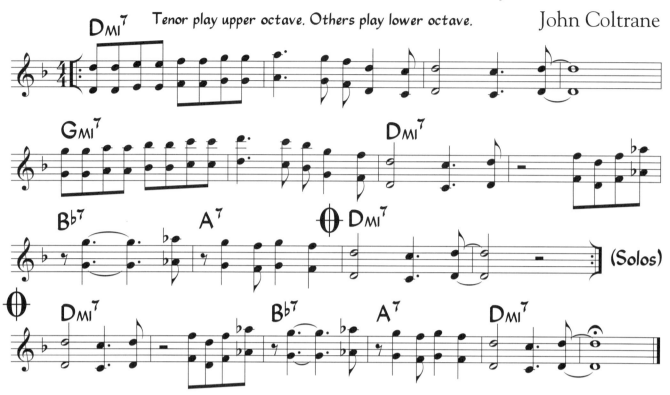

Mr. P.C. is a 12-bar minor blues. Segments of the motivic melody are transposed to match the chord changes. It was originally played with a fast swing feel.

On Cue: Background for solos. (Duplicates Part 2) Tenor play upper octave. Others play lower octave.

Shout chorus (3 parts). Play after solos (optional). All play as written.

D.C. al Coda

Supplemental Material - Mr. P.C.

Sample Piano Voicings

Basic 3-note voicings   Rootless voicings

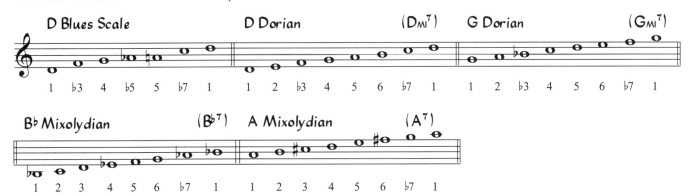

Useful Scales

Sample Bass Line

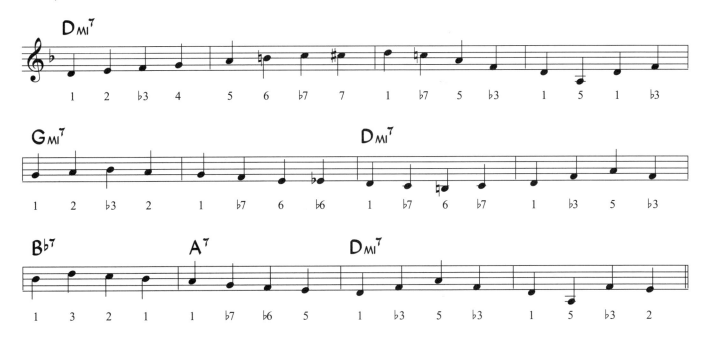

Mr. P.C. (Part 2 - harmony)

Tenor play upper octave. Others play lower octave.

(Solos)

On Cue: Background for solos. Tenor play upper octave. Others play lower octave.

Shout chorus. All play single notes. For octs: Tenor play upper notes. Others play lower notes.

D.C. al Coda

Useful scales:

D Blues Scale

D Dorian (DMI7)

G Dorian (GMI7)

Bb Mixolydian (Bb7)

A Mixolydian (A7)

Mr. P.C. (Part 3 - harmony)

Useful scales:

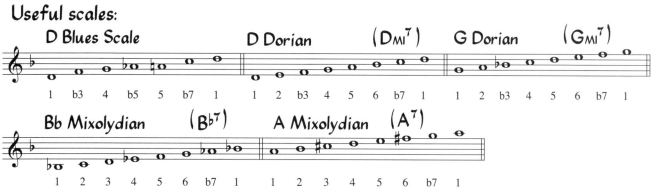

One for Daddy-O (Part 1 - melody)

Nat Adderley

One For Daddy-O is a 12-bar minor blues. This was originally played with a medium-slow swing feel. On the head, no chord is played in bars 5 and 6. Alternatively, use C7(#9) instead of Cmi7 and F7(#9) instead of Fmi7 chord, on the head only.

On Cue: Background for solos. (Duplicates Part 2) Tenor play upper notes, Others play lower notes.

Shout chorus Play after solos (optional). All play this part.

D.S. al Coda

Supplemental Material - One For Daddy-O

Sample Piano Voicings

Basic 3-note voicings

	CMI7	C7	FMI7	DMI7(b5)	G7
	b7	b7	b3	b3	b7
	b3	3	b7	b7	3
	1	1	1	1	1

Rootless voicings

	CMI7	C7	FMI7	DMI7(b5)	G7
	9	9	5	b7	5
	b7	b7	b3	b5	3
	b3	3	b7	b3	b7

Useful Scales

C Dorian (CMI7)

1	2	b3	4	5	6	b7	1

C Blues Scale

1	b3	4	b5	5	b7	1

Sample Bass Line

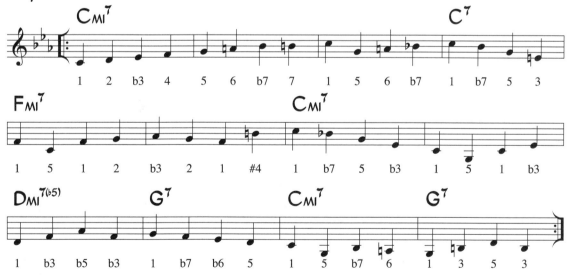

CMI7 ... C7

1	2	b3	4	5	6	b7	7	1	5	6	b7	1	b7	5	3

FMI7 ... CMI7

1	5	1	2	b3	2	1	#4	1	b7	5	b3	1	5	1	b3

DMI7(b5) ... G7 ... CMI7 ... G7

1	b3	b5	b3	1	b7	b6	5	1	5	b7	6	1	3	5	3

92

One for Daddy-O (Part 2 - harmony)

93

One for Daddy-O (Part 3 - harmony)

Tenor play upper notes, Others play lower notes.

On Cue: Background for solos. Tenor play upper notes, Others play lower notes.

Shout chorus Play after solos (optional). Tenor play upper note, others play lower note.

D.S. al Fine

Useful scales:

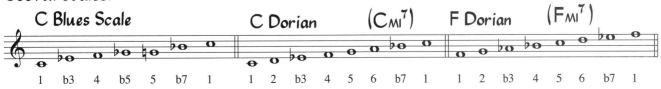

C Blues Scale   C Dorian (C Mi⁷)   F Dorian (F Mi⁷)

94

Red's Good Groove (Part 1 - melody)

Red Garland

All play single notes. For octs: Tenor play upper notes. Others play lower notes.

(Solos)

Red's Good Groove is a 12-bar blues. It was originally played with a slow swing feel.

On Cue: Background for solos. (Duplicates Part 2) Tenor play upper octave. Others play lower octave.

Shout chorus (3 parts). Play after solos (optional). All play as written.

D.S. al Coda

Supplemental Material - Red's Good Groove

Sample Piano Voicings

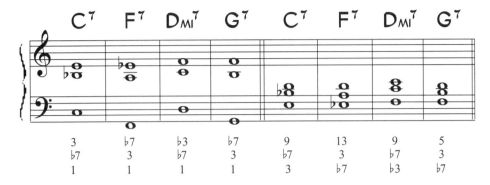

Useful Scales

Sample Bass Line

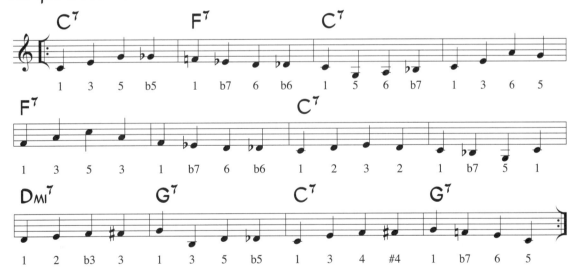

96

Red's Good Groove (Part 2 - harmony)

Tenor play upper octave. Others play lower octave.

(Solos)

On Cue: Background for solos. Tenor play upper octave. Others play lower octave.

Shout chorus. All play single notes. For octs: Tenor play upper notes. Others play lower notes.

D.S. al Coda

Useful scales: C Blues Scale

1   b3   4   b5   5   b7   1

Red's Good Groove (Part 3 - harmony)

Tenor play upper octave. Others play lower octave.

(Solos)

On Cue: Background for solos. Tenor play upper octave. Others play lower octave.

Shout chorus. All play single notes. For octs: Tenor play upper notes. Others play lower notes.

D.S. al Coda

Useful scales: C Blues Scale

1   b3   4   b5   5   b7   1

98

Revelation (Part 1 - melody)

Kenny Barron

All play single notes. For octs: Tenor play upper notes. Others play lower notes.

Revelation is a 12-bar minor blues with a motivic melody. It was originally played with a medium-swing feel.

On Cue: Background for solos. (Duplicates Part 2) Tenor play upper octave. Others play lower octave.

Shout chorus (3 parts). Play after solos (optional). All play as written.

©1961 Wazuri Publishing Co. Renewed. Used by Permission

Supplemental Material - Revelation

Sample Piano Voicings

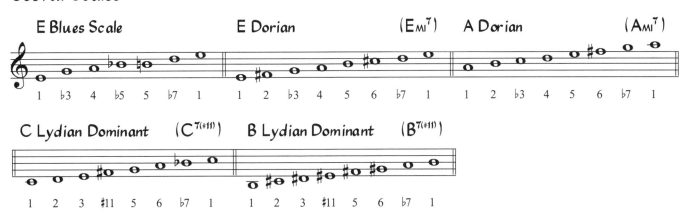

Useful Scales

Sample Bass Line

100

Revelation (Part 2 - harmony)

Tenor play upper octave. Others play lower octave.

On Cue: Background for solos. Tenor play upper octave. Others play lower octave.

Shout chorus. Tenor play upper octave. Others play lower octave.

D.S. al Coda

Useful scales:

Revelation (Part 3 - harmony)

All play single notes. For octs: Tenor play upper notes. Others play lower notes.

Road Song (Part 1 - melody)

John L. ("Wes") Montgomery

Road Song has a 32-bar AABA form. It was originally played with a straight-eighth feel. For solos, disregard the E7(#9) in bar 8 of each A section.

On Cue: Background for solos. Tenor play upper octave. Others play lower octave.

(after solos)
D.S. al Fine

Supplemental Material - Road Song

Sample Piano Voicings

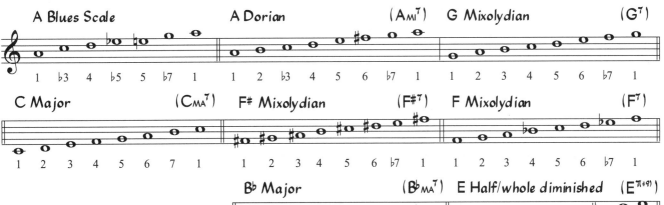

Useful Scales

Sample Bass Line

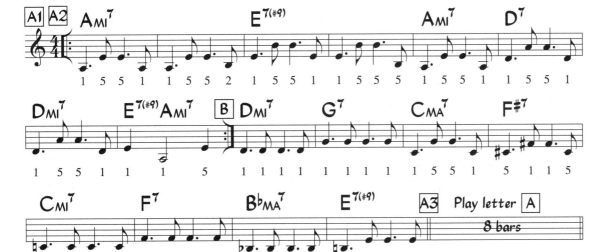

104

Road Song (Part 2 - harmony)

For solos, disregard the E7(#9) in bar 8 of each A section.

On Cue: Background for solos. Tenor play upper octave. Others play lower octave.

(after solos)
D.S. al Fine

Useful scales:

A Dorian (A_{MI}^{7}) G Mixolydian (G^{7}) C Major (C_{MA}^{7}) F# Mixolydian $(F^{\#7})$

1 2 b3 4 5 6 b7 1   1 2 3 4 5 6 b7 1   1 2 3 4 5 6 7 1   1 2 3 4 5 6 b7 1

F Mixolydian (F^{7}) Bb Major $(B^{b}_{MA}{}^{7})$ E half/whole dimin. $(E^{7(\#9)})$

1 2 3 4 5 6 b7 1   1 2 3 4 5 6 7 1   1 b2 b3 3 b5 5 6 b7 1

Road Song (Part 3 - harmony)

Short Stuff (Part 1 - melody)

Cedar Walton

Short Stuff has an 8-bar form with a descending turnaround. It was originally played with a medium-slow swing feel.

On Cue: Background for solos. (Duplicates Part 2) Tenor play upper octave. Others play lower octave.

Shout chorus. All play single notes. For octs: Tenor play upper note. Others play lower note.

Supplemental Material - Short Stuff

Sample Piano Voicings

Basic 3-note voicings   Rootless voicings

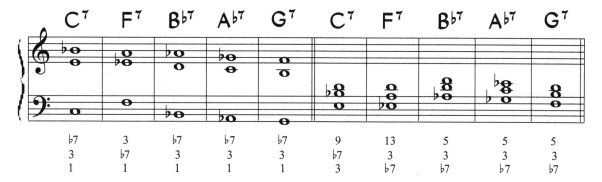

Useful Scales

C Blues Scale

Sample Bass Line

Short Stuff (Part 2 - harmony)

Tenor play upper octave. Others play lower octave.

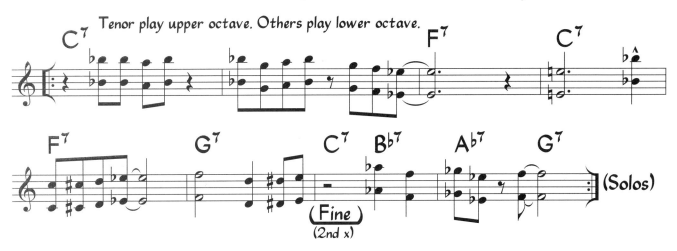

On Cue: Background for solos. Tenor play upper octave. Others play lower octave.

Shout chorus. Play after solos (optional). Tenor play upper octave. Others play lower octave.

D.C. al Fine
(with repeat)

Useful scales:

C Blues Scale

1   b3   4   b5   5   b7   1

Short Stuff (Part 3 - harmony)

All play single notes. For octs: Tenor play upper note, Others play lower note.

(Solos)

(Fine)
(2nd x)

Background for solos. All play single notes. For octs: Tenor play upper notes, Others play lower note.

Shout chorus. All play single notes. For octs: Tenor play upper note. Others play lower note.

D.C. al Fine
(with repeat)

Useful scales:

C Blues Scale

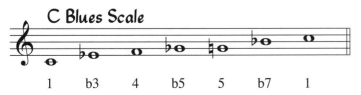

| 1 | b3 | 4 | b5 | 5 | b7 | 1 |

Shoshana (Part 1 - melody)

Mark Levine

Shoshana features a rhythmic piano part called a "montuno." Other instruments can play this for arrangement purposes. This song was originally played with a straight-eighth feel. Solos are over the A section only. The B section is written to be an interlude. It is a single-line melody.

On Cue: Background for solos. (Duplicates Part 2)
Tenor play upper notes. Others play lower notes.

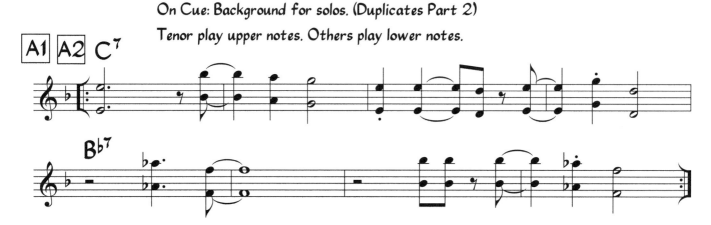

Supplemental Material - Shoshana

Sample Piano Voicings

Basic 3-note voicings   Rootless voicings

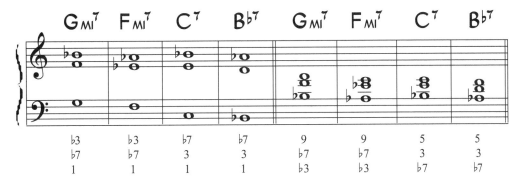

Useful Scales

Sample Bass Line

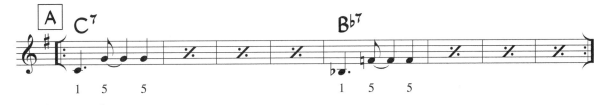

(montuno)

112

Shoshana (Part 2 - harmony)

Shoshana features a rhythmic piano part called a "montuno." Other instruments can play this for arrangement purposes. This song was originally played with a straight-eighth feel. Solos are over the A section only. The B section is written to be an interlude. It is a single-line melody.

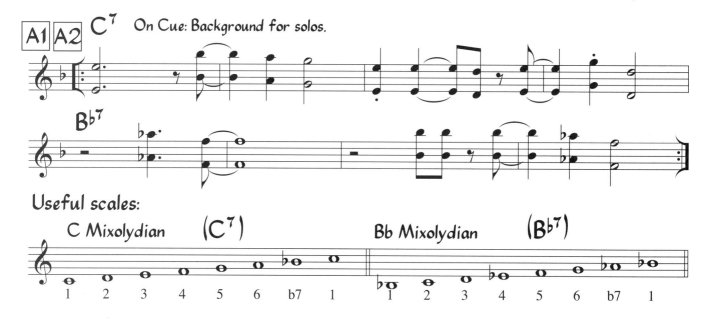

Shoshana (Part 3 - harmony)

Shoshana features a rhythmic piano part called a "montuno." Other instruments can play this for arrangement purposes. This song was originally played with a straight-eighth feel. Solos are over the A section only. The B section is written to be an interlude. It is a single-line melody.

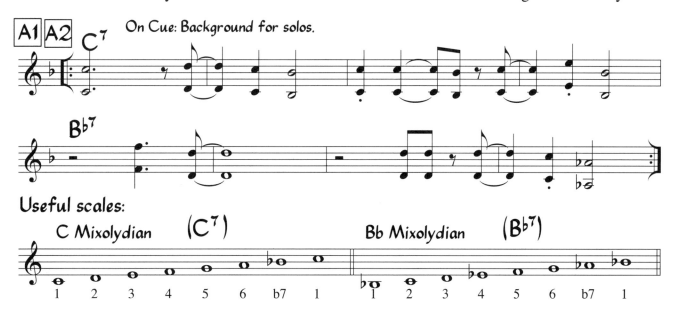

Sir John (Part 1 - melody)

Blue Mitchell

Sir John is a 12-bar blues. It was originally played with a medium-swing feel.
The Eb6 chord in bar 2 should be played as Eb7 during solos.

On Cue: Background for solos. (Duplicates Part 2) Tenor play upper octave. Others play lower octave.

Shout chorus (3 parts). Play after solos (optional). All play as written.

D.S. al Coda

Supplemental Material - Sir John

Sample Piano Voicings

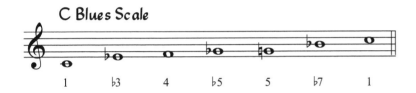

Useful Scales

Sample Bass Line

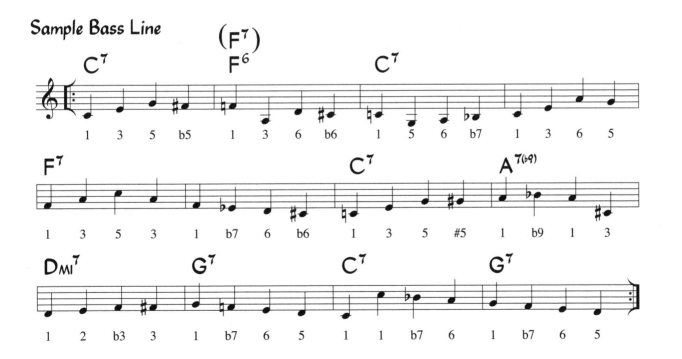

Sir John (Part 2 - harmony)

Tenor play upper octave.

Others play lower octave.

(Solos)

On Cue: Background for solos. Tenor play upper notes. Others play lower notes.

Shout chorus. Tenor play upper notes. Others play lower notes.

D.S. al Coda

Useful scales: C Blues Scale

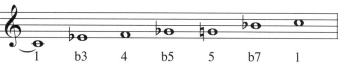

Sir John (Part 3 - harmony)

All play single notes. For octs, Tenor play
upper note, Others play lower note.

(Solos)

Background for solos. All play single notes. For octs, Tenor play upper note, Others play lower note.

Shout chorus. All play single notes. For octs: Tenor play upper note. Others play lower note.

D.S. al Coda

Useful scales: C Blues Scale

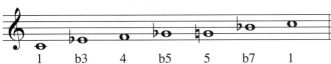

1   b3   4   b5   5   b7   1

Sister Sadie (Part 1 - melody)

Tenor play upper notes, others play lower notes.

(For Solos, primarily just A7 for the A sectionns.)

Horace Silver

(1st x only)

(Solos)

low A

Sister Sadie has a 32-bar AABA form. The melody is accompanied by stop-time hits from the rhythm section. It was originally recorded with a medium-swing feel.

Unison Background for solos is in Parts 2 and 3.

Supplemental Material - Sister Sadie

Sample Piano Voicings

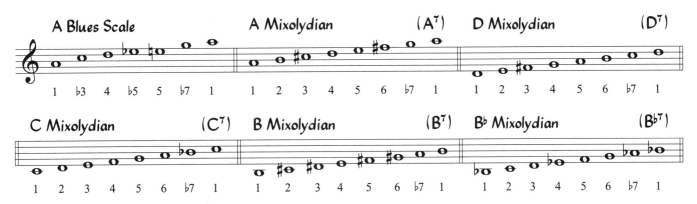

Useful Scales

Sample Bass Line

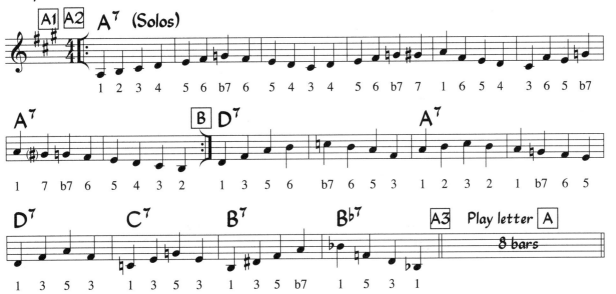

Sister Sadie (Part 2 - harmony)

Sister Sadie (Part 3 - harmony)

So Danço Samba (Part 1 - melody)

Antonio Carlos Jobim

Só Danço Samba is a 32-bar tune with an AABA form. It has a similar chord progression to Billy Strayhorn's Take The A Train. This song was originally played with a straight-eighth feel.

On Cue: Background for solos. Tenor play upper notes, others play lower notes.

(after solos)
D.S. al Coda

Supplemental Material - Só Danço Samba

Sample Piano Voicings

Basic 3-note voicings **Rootless voicings**

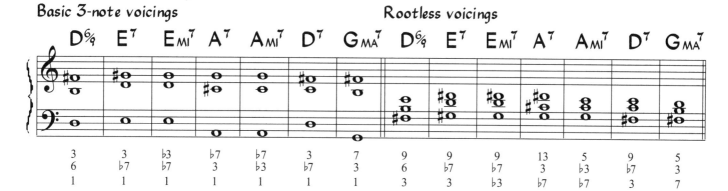

Useful Scales

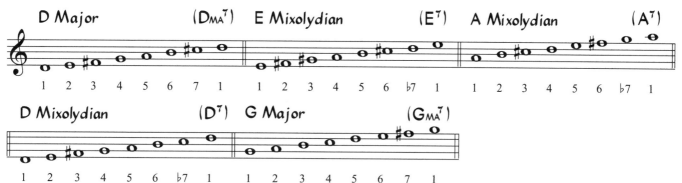

Sample Bass Line

So Danço Samba (Part 2 - harmony)

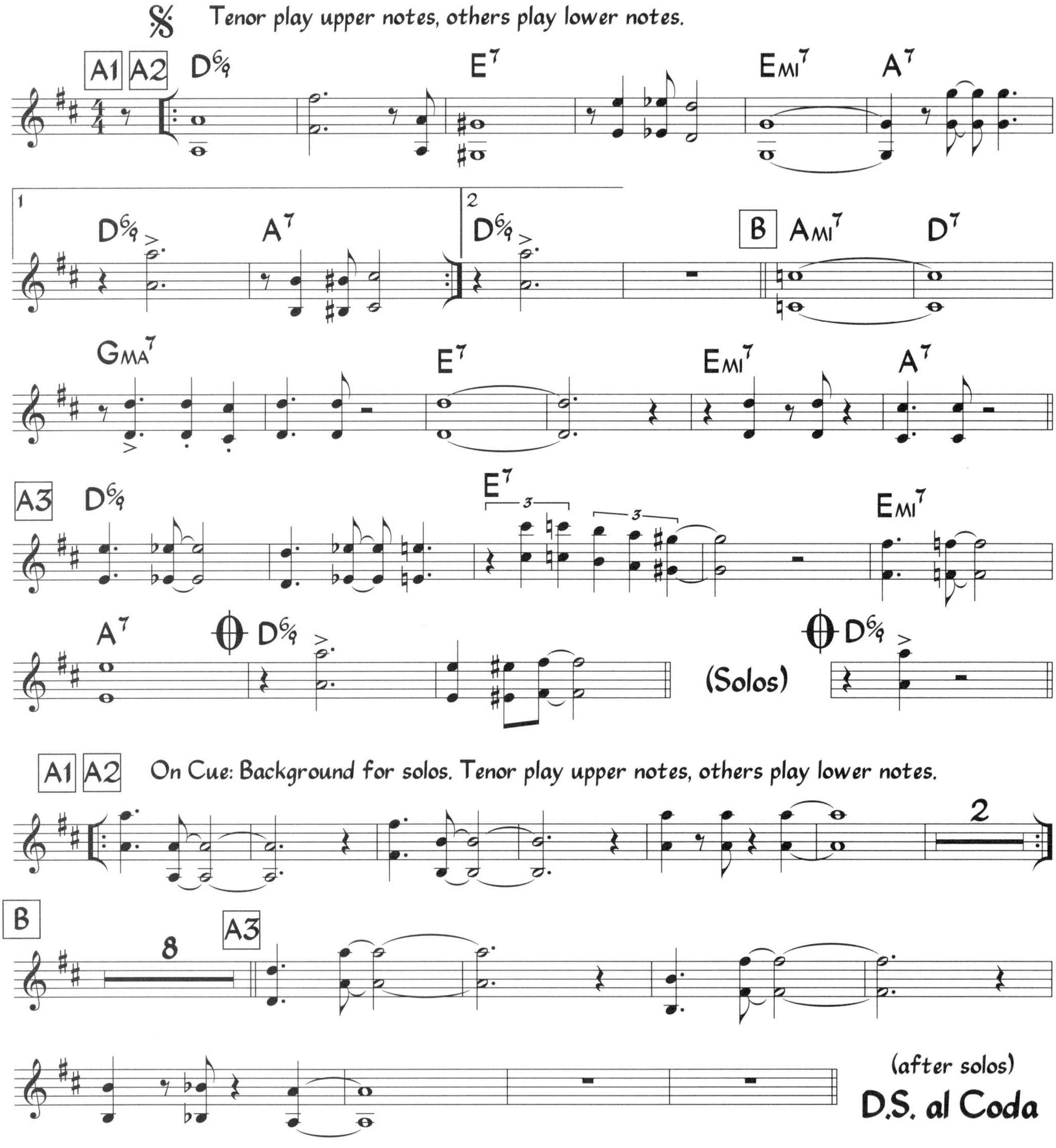

Useful scales:

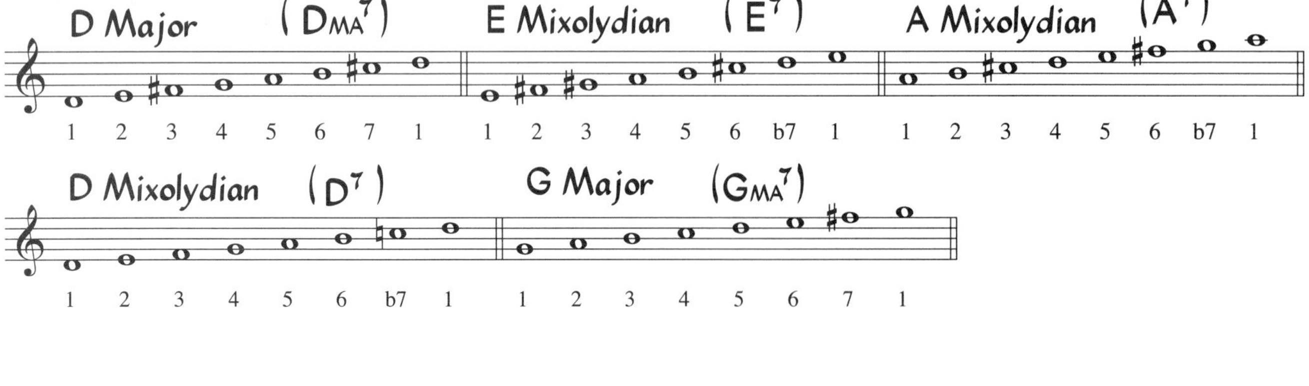

So Danço Samba (Part 3 - harmony)

𝄋 Tenor play upper notes, others play lower notes.

A1 A2 D⁶⁄₉ E⁷ Emi⁷ A⁷

1. D⁶⁄₉ A⁷ 2. D⁶⁄₉ B Ami⁷ D⁷

Gma⁷ E⁷ Emi⁷ A⁷

A3 D⁶⁄₉ E⁷ Emi⁷

A⁷ ⊕D⁶⁄₉ (Solos) ⊕D⁶⁄₉

A1 A2 On Cue: Background for solos. Tenor play upper notes, others play lower notes.

2

B 8 A3

(after solos)
D.S. al Coda

Useful scales:

D Major (Dma⁷) E Mixolydian (E⁷) A Mixolydian (A⁷)

1 2 3 4 5 6 7 1   1 2 3 4 5 6 b7 1   1 2 3 4 5 6 b7 1

D Mixolydian (D⁷) G Major (Gma⁷)

1 2 3 4 5 b7 1   1 2 3 4 5 6 7 1

Song for My Father (Part 1 - melody)

Horace Silver

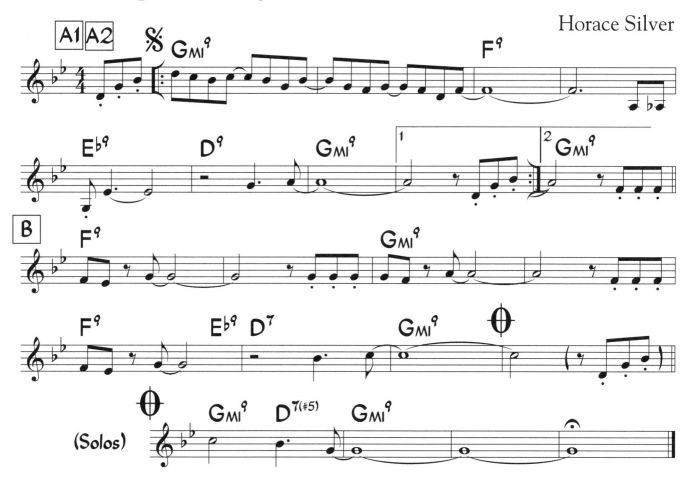

Song For My Father has an AAB form. It is common for the pianist to double
the bass line during the melody. It was originally played with a straight-eighth feel.

Supplemental Material - Song For My Father

Sample Piano Voicings

Basic 3-note voicings   Rootless voicings

Useful Scales

Sample Bass Line

128

Song for My Father (Part 2 - harmony)

Song for My Father (Part 3 - harmony)

Sonnymoon for Two (Part 1 - melody)

Sonny Rollins

(Solos)

Sonnymoon For Two is a 12-bar blues with a repeating motivic melody that doesn't change to match the chords. This was originally played with a medium-swing feel.

On Cue: Background for solos. (Duplicates Part 2) Tenor play upper octave. Others play lower octave.

Shout chorus. Play after solos (optional). Tenor play upper octave. Others play lower octave.

D.C. al Coda

Supplemental Material - Sonnymoon For Two

Sample Piano Voicings

Basic 3-note voicings   Rootless voicings

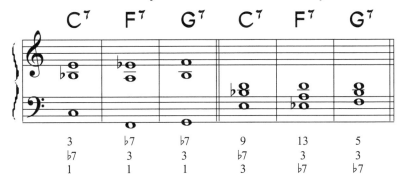

Useful Scales

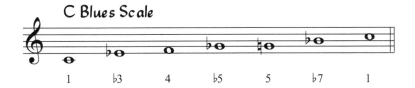

Sample Bass Line

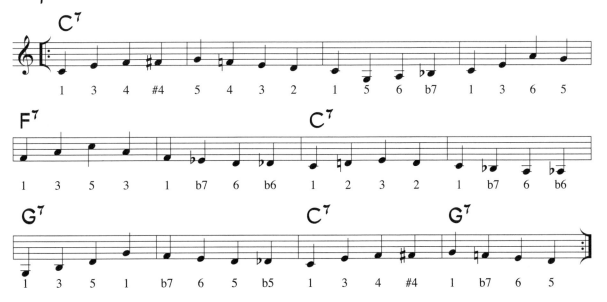

Sonnymoon for Two (Part 2 - harmony)

Tenor play upper octave. Others play lower octave.

(Solos)

On Cue: Background for solos. Tenor play upper notes. Others play lower notes.

Shout chorus. Play after solos (optional). Tenor play upper octave. Others play lower octave.

D.C. al Coda

Useful scales: C Blues Scale

1   b3   4   b5   5   b7   1

Sonnymoon for Two (Part 3 - harmony)

(Solos)

On Cue: Background for solos. Tenor play upper notes. Others play lower notes.

Shout chorus. All play single notes. For octs: Tenor play upper note. Others play lower note.

D.C. al Coda

Useful scales: C Blues Scale

1   b3   4   b5   5   b7   1

St. James Infirmary (Part 1 - melody)

Tenor play upper notes, Others play lower notes.

Joe Primrose

Saint James Infirmary is usually played with a slow-swing feel.

On Cue: Background for solos. (Duplicates Part 2) Tenor play upper notes. Others play lower notes.

Shout chorus (optional). All play single notes. For octs:
Tenor play upper note. Others play lower note.

D.S. al Coda

Supplemental Material - Saint James Infirmary

Sample Piano Voicings

Basic 3-note voicings   **Rootless voicings**

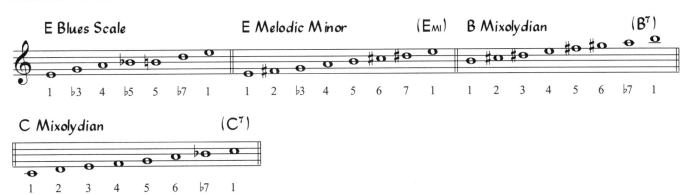

Emi	B7	C7	B7	Emi	B7	C7	B7
b3	3	3	b7	9	5	3	3
5	b7	b7	3	6	3	b7	b7
1	1	1	1	b3	b7	5	5

Useful Scales

E Blues Scale   E Melodic Minor   (Emi)   B Mixolydian   (B7)

1	b3	4	b5	5	b7	1

1	2	b3	4	5	6	7	1

1	2	3	4	5	6	b7	1

C Mixolydian   (C7)

1	2	3	4	5	6	b7	1

Sample Bass Line

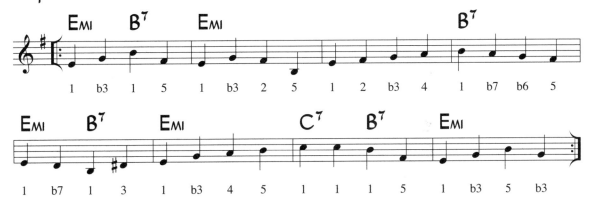

Emi		B7		Emi								B7			
1	b3	1	5	1	b3	2	5	1	2	b3	4	1	b7	b6	5

Emi		B7		Emi				C7		B7		Emi			
1	b7	1	3	1	b3	4	5	1	1	1	5	1	b3	5	b3

136

St. James Infirmary (Part 2 - harmony)

Tenor play upper notes, Others play lower notes.

(Solos)

On Cue: Background for solos. Tenor play upper notes. Others play lower notes.

Shout chorus (optional). All play single notes. For octs:

Tenor play upper note. Others play lower note.

D.S. al Coda

Useful scales:

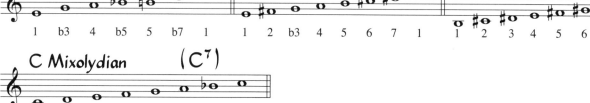

St. James Infirmary (Part 3 - harmony)

All play single notes. For octs: Tenor play upper notes. Others play lower notes.

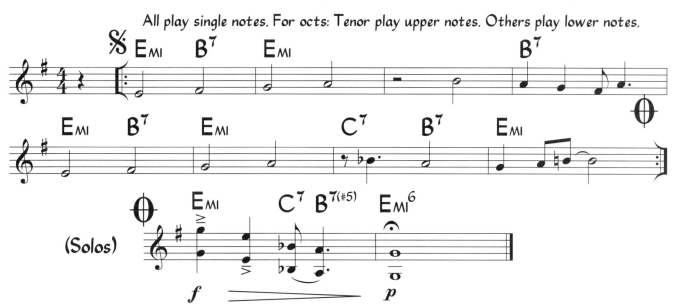

(Solos)

On Cue: Background for solos. Tenor play upper notes. Others play lower notes.

Shout chorus (optional). Tenor play upper notes, Others play lower notes.

D.S. al Coda

Useful scales:

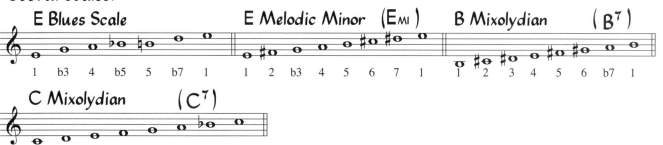

St. Thomas (Part 1 - melody)

Sonny Rollins

St. Thomas was originally played with a straight-eighth feel.

On Cue: Background for solos. (Duplicates Part 2) Tenor play upper octave. Others play lower octave.

Shout chorus (3 parts). Play after solos (optional). All play single notes as written.

For octaves: Tenor play upper note, others play lower note.

Supplemental Material - St. Thomas

Sample Piano Voicings

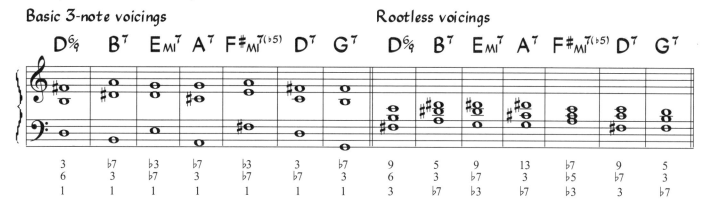

Useful Scales

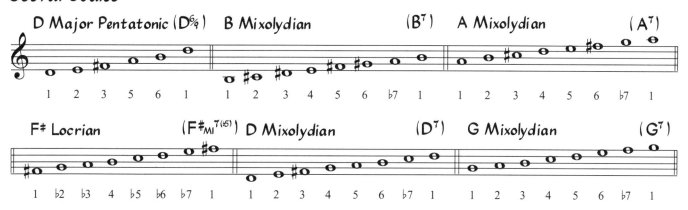

Sample Bass Line

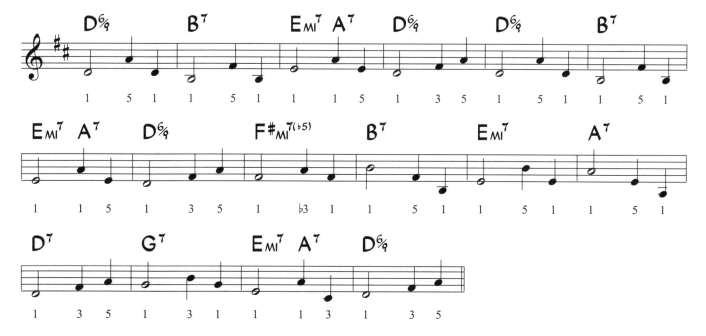

St. Thomas (Part 2 - harmony)

St. Thomas (Part 3 - harmony)

Straight Life (Part 1 - melody)

Freddie Hubbard

(Solos)

Straight Life has a simple melody based on scales.
It was originally played with a straight-eighth feel.

On Cue: Background for solos. Tenor play upper notes, others play lower notes.

(after solos)

D.S. al Coda

(with pick-ups)

Supplemental Material - Straight Life

Sample Piano Voicings

Basic 3-note voicings   Rootless voicings

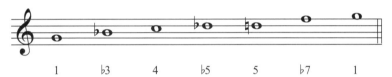

3	3	9	9
b7	b7	b7	b7
1	1	3	3

Useful Scales

G Blues Scale

1   b3   4   b5   5   b7   1

Sample Bass Line

G⁷   F⁷

1   1   b7   1   1   7   1   1   b7   1   #1   2

Straight Life (Part 2 - harmony)

Tenor play upper notes, others play lower notes.

(Solos)

On Cue: Background for solos. Tenor play upper notes, others play lower notes.

(after solos)

D.S. al Coda

(with pick-ups)

Useful scales:

G Blues Scale

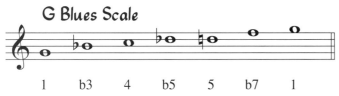

1   b3   4   b5   5   b7   1

Straight Life (Part 3 - harmony)

All play single lines. For octs: Tenor play upper note, others play lower note,

(Solos)

On Cue: Background for solos. Tenor play upper notes, others play lower notes.

(after solos)

D.S. al Coda
(with pick-ups)

Useful scales:
G Blues Scale

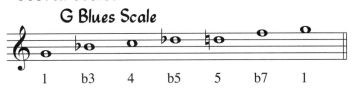

1   b3   4   b5   5   b7   1

Tenor Madness (Part 1 - melody)

Sonny Rollins

Tenor Madness is a 12-bar blues with a bebop melody. It was originally played with a medium-fast swing feel.

On Cue: Background for solos. (Duplicates Part 2) Tenor play upper notes. Others play lower notes.

Shout chorus. All play single notes. For octs: Tenor play upper note. Others play lower note.

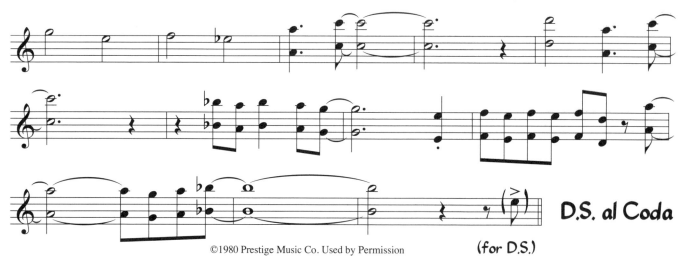

D.S. al Coda

(for D.S.)

Supplemental Material - Tenor Madness

Sample Piano Voicings

Basic 3-note voicings   Rootless voicings

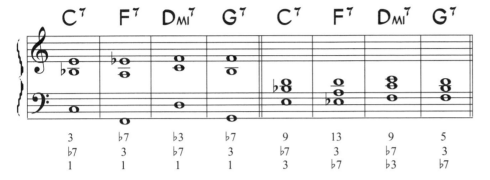

Useful Scales

Sample Bass Line

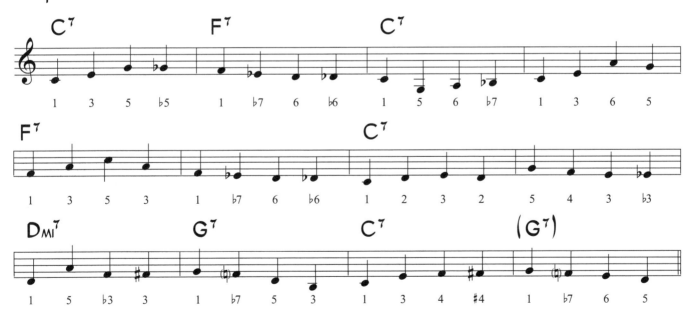

Tenor Madness (Part 2 - harmony)

All play single notes. For octs, Tenor play upper note, Others play lower note.

On Cue: Background for solos. Tenor play upper notes. Others play lower notes.

Shout chorus. Play after solos (optional). Tenor play upper octave. Others play lower octave.

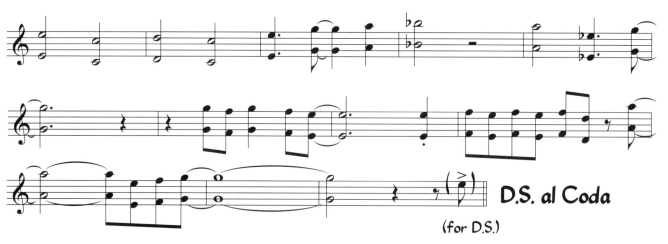

D.S. al Coda

(for D.S.)

Useful scales: C Blues Scale

1   b3   4   b5   5   b7   1

Tenor Madness (Part 3 - harmony)

All play as written.

On Cue: Background for solos. Tenor play upper notes. Others play lower notes.

Shout chorus. All play single notes. For octs: Tenor play upper note. Others play lower note.

D.S. al Coda

Useful scales: C Blues Scale

Trail Dust (Part 1 - melody)

Jim Rotondi

Trail Dust was originally played with a medium-swing feel.

On Cue: Background for solos. (Duplicates Part 2) Tenor play upper notes. Others play lower notes.

Shout chorus. All play single notes. For octs: Tenor play upper note. Others play lower note.

D.S. al Coda

Supplemental Material - Trail Dust

Sample Piano Voicings

Basic 3-note voicings

Rootless voicings

Useful Scales

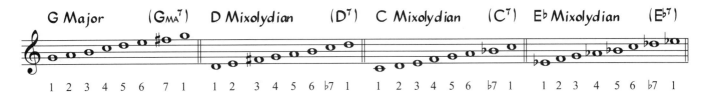

Sample Bass Line

152

Trail Dust (Part 2 - harmony)

Trail Dust (Part 3 - harmony)

All play single notes. For octs, Tenor play upper note, Others play lower note.

On Cue: Background for solos. Tenor play upper notes. Others play lower notes.

Shout chorus. All play single notes. For octs: Tenor play upper note. Others play lower note.

D.S. al Coda

Useful scales:

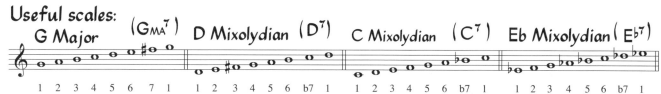

When the Saints Go Marching In
(Part 1 - melody)

Traditional

When The Saints Go Marching In is usually played with a medium-swing feel.

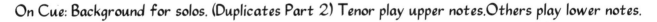

On Cue: Background for solos. (Duplicates Part 2) Tenor play upper notes. Others play lower notes.

(after solos)

D.S. al Coda

(with pick-ups)

Supplemental Material - When The Saints Go Marching In

Sample Piano Voicings

Useful Scales

Sample Bass Line

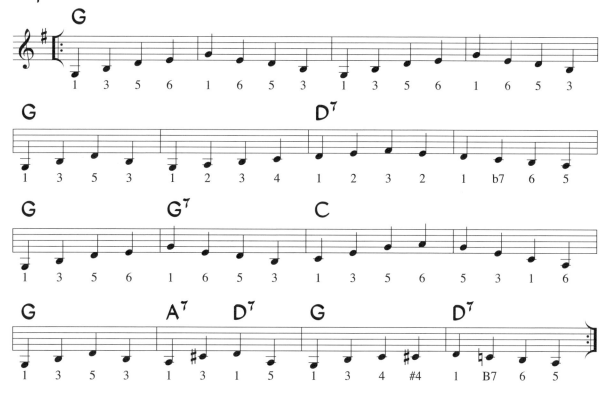

When the Saints Go Marching In
(Part 2 - harmony)

Tenor play upper notes. Others play lower notes.

(Solos)

On Cue: Background for solos. Tenor play upper notes. Others play lower notes.

(after solos)
D.S. al Coda
(with pick-ups)

Useful scales:
G Major Pentatonic (G)   C Major Pentatonic (C)   D Mixolydian (D⁷)

1 2 3 5 6 1   1 2 3 5 6 1   1 2 3 4 5 6 b7 1

When the Saints Go Marching In
(Part 3 - harmony)

All play single notes. For octs, Tenor play upper note, Others play lower note.

(Solos)

On Cue: Background for solos. All play single notes. For octs, Tenor play upper note, Others play lower note.

(after solos)
D.S. al Coda
(with pick-ups)

Useful scales:

G Major Pentatonic (G)   C Major Pentatonic (C)   D Mixolydian   (D⁷)

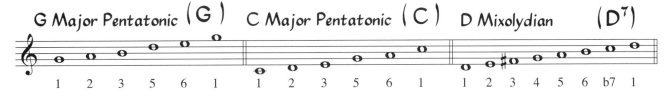

1 2 3 5 6 1   1 2 3 5 6 1   1 2 3 4 5 6 b7 1

Work Song (Part 1 - melody)

Nat Adderley

(Solos)

(after solos)

D.C. al Coda

Disregard breaks and figures during solos.

Background for solos is included on 2nd and 3rd parts.

Work Song has a 16 bar form and a call and response melody.
It was originally played with a medium swing feel.

Supplemental Material - Work Song

Sample Piano Voicings

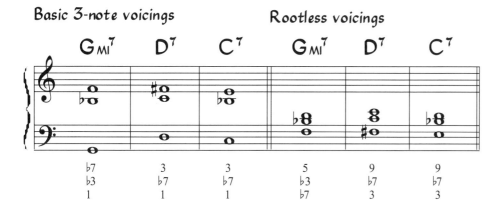

Useful Scales

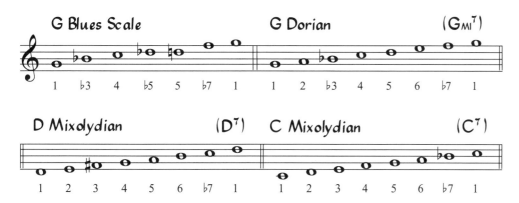

Sample Bass Line

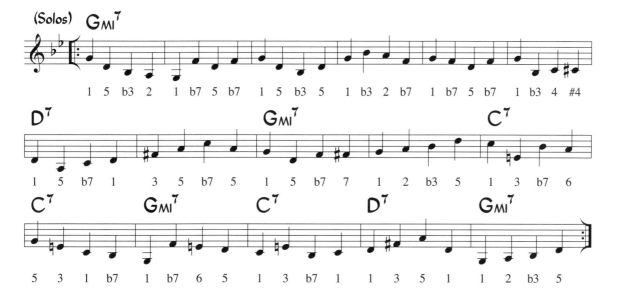

Work Song (Part 2 - harmony)

Work Song (Part 3 - harmony)

Yardbird Suite (Part 1 - melody)

Charlie Parker

All play single lines. For octaves: Tenor play upper note, others play lower note.

Yardbird Suite has a 32-bar AABA form and a bebop melody. It was originally played with a medium-fast swing feel.

On Cue: Background for solos. Tenor play upper notes, others play lower notes.

(after solos)

D.C. al Coda

Supplemental Material - Yardbird Suite

Sample Piano Voicings

Basic 3-note voicings

Rootless voicings

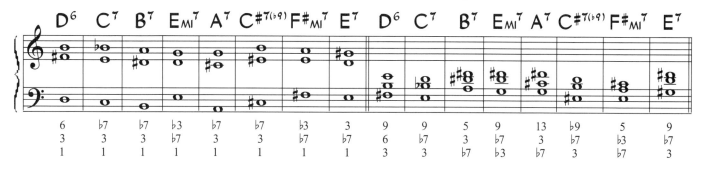

Useful Scales

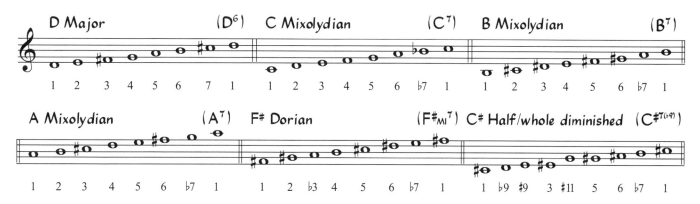

Sample Bass Line

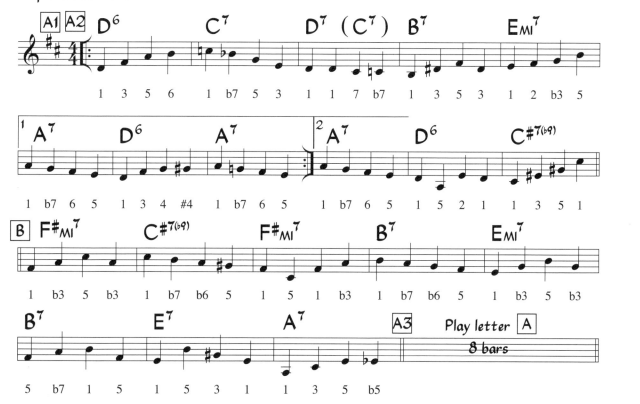

Yardbird Suite (Part 2 - harmony)

Yardbird Suite (Part 3 - harmony)

Z's Blues (Part 1 - melody)

Eric Alexander

Z's Blues is a 12-bar blues that was originally played with a medium-swing feel.

On Cue: Background for solos. (Duplicates Part 2) Tenor play upper notes, Others play lower notes.

Shout chorus. Play after solos (optional). Tenor play upper octave. Others play lower octave.

Supplemental Material - Z's Blues

Sample Piano Voicings

Basic 3-note voicings

C⁷	G⁷	F#⁷	F⁷	F#°	A⁷⁽♭⁹⁾	D_MI⁷

♭7	3	3	3	♭3	♭7	♭3
3	♭7	♭7	♭7	♭♭7	3	♭7
1	1	1	1	1	1	1

Root and rootless voicings

C⁷	G⁷	F#⁷	F⁷	F#°	A⁷⁽♭⁹⁾	D_MI⁷

9	5	13	13	♭5	3	9
♭7	3	3	3	♭3	♭9	♭7
3	♭7	♭7	♭7	♭♭7	♭7	♭3

Useful Scales

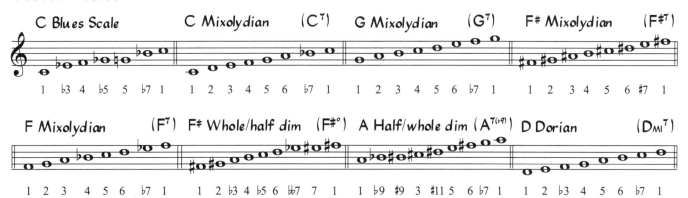

C Blues Scale — 1 ♭3 4 ♭5 5 ♭7 1

C Mixolydian (C⁷) — 1 2 3 4 5 6 ♭7 1

G Mixolydian (G⁷) — 1 2 3 4 5 6 ♭7 1

F# Mixolydian (F#⁷) — 1 2 3 4 5 6 #7 1

F Mixolydian (F⁷) — 1 2 3 4 5 6 ♭7 1

F# Whole/half dim (F#°) — 1 2 ♭3 4 ♭5 6 ♭♭7 7 1

A Half/whole dim (A⁷⁽♭⁹⁾) — 1 ♭9 #9 3 #11 5 6 ♭7 1

D Dorian (D_MI⁷) — 1 2 ♭3 4 5 6 ♭7 1

Sample Bass Line

C⁷				G⁷				C⁷				F#⁷				F⁷				F#°			

1 3 5 6 | 1 3 ♭7 1 | 1 ♭7 6 5 | 1 3 1 ♭7 | 1 3 5 3 | 1 ♭3 ♭5 ♭3

C⁷ / A⁷⁽♭⁹⁾ / D_MI⁷ / G⁷ / C⁷ / G⁷

5 ♭7 1 ♭7 | 1 ♭7 5 3 | 1 2 ♭3 5 | 1 ♭7 6 5 | 1 3 6 ♭6 | 1 ♭7 6 5

Z's Blues (Part 2 - harmony)

Tenor play upper notes, Others play lower notes.

On Cue: Background for solos. Tenor play upper notes. Others play lower notes.

Shout chorus. All play single notes. For octs: Tenor play upper note. Others play lower note.

Useful scales:

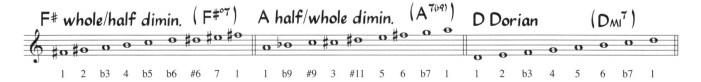

Z's Blues (Part 3 - harmony)

Tenor play upper notes, Others play lower notes.

On Cue: Background for solos. Tenor play upper notes. Others play lower notes.

Shout chorus. All play single notes. For octs: Tenor play upper note. Others play lower note.

Useful scales:

Appendix I - Additional Educational Material

Chords and Complementary Scales

Cycle of Fifths

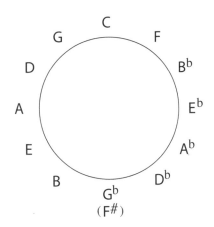
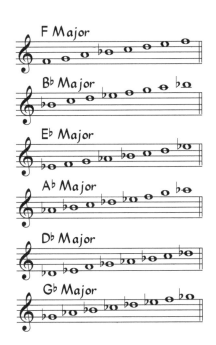

Move clockwise down a fifth, move counterclockwise up a fifth.

Transposing A Riff

Basic Drum Patterns

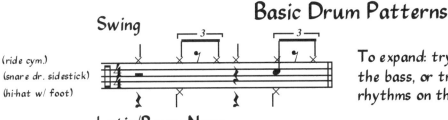

Swing

To expand: try playing light quarter notes on the bass, or try improvising different comping rhythms on the snare.

Latin/Bossa Nova

To expand: play the ride cymbal pattern on the (closed) hi-hat.

Rock/Funk

You can try varying the bass drum pattern, opening and closing the hi-hat, or playing the hi-hat pattern on the ride cymbal when appropriate.

Jazz Waltz

To expand: try playing light quarter notes on the bass, or try improvising different comping rhythms on the snare.

Appendix II - Discography

Below are the original &/or most well-known versions of the tunes in THE REAL EASY BOOK. You will definitely benefit by listening to how the masters play this material!

1. Bags' Groove . . . . .Miles Davis' "Bags' Groove"; MJQ's "Modern Jazz Quartet:1957"
2. Big Bertha . . . . Duke Pearson's "Sweey Honey Bee"
3. Blue Seven . . . . Sonny Rollins' "Saxophone Colossus"
4. Blues By Five . . . . Miles Davis' "Cookin' With The Miles Davis Quintet"
5. Blues In The Closet . . . . Bud Powell's "Blues In The Closet"
6. Cold Duck Time . . . . Les McCann & Eddie Harris' "Swiss Movement"
7. Contemplation . . . . McCoy Tyner's "The Real McCoy"
8. Doxy . . . . Miles Davis' "Bags' Groove"; "Sonny Rollins And The Big Brass"
9. Edward Lee . . . . "Eric Alexander Quartet Live At The Keynote"
10. Equinox . . . . .John Coltrane's "Coltrane's Sound"
11. Freedom Jazz Dance . . . . "The Best Of Eddie Harris"; Miles Davis' "Miles Smiles"
12. Gingerbread Boy . . . . Miles Davis' "Miles Smiles"; Jimmy Heath Quintet's "On The Trail"
13. Groove Merchant . . . . .Jerome Richardson's "Jazz Station Runaway", Thad Jones/Mel Lewis Orchestra's "Basle 1969"
14. Jive Samba . . . . Cannonball Adderley's "Dizzy's Business"
15. Jo Jo Calypso . . . . .Not currently recorded
17. Killer Joe . . . . Art Farmer/Benny Golson & The Jazztet's "Meet The Jazztet"
18. Listen Here . . . . "The Best Of Eddie Harris"
19. Little Sunflower . . . . Freddie Hubbard's "Backlash"
20. Mercy, Mercy, Mercy . . . . Cannonball Adderley's "Mercy, Mercy, Mercy"
21. Midnight Waltz . . . . Cedar Walton's "Among Friends"
22. Mr. P.C . . . . John Coltrane's "Giant Steps"
23. One For Daddy-O . . . . Cannonball Adderley's "Somethin' Else"
24. Red's Good Groove . . . . Red Garland's "Red's Good Groove"
25. Revelation . . . . .Yusef Lateef's "The Centaur And The Phoenix"
26. Road Song . . . . "Wes Montgomery's Finest Hour"
27. Short Stuff . . . . Cedar Walton's "Cedar!"
28. Shoshana . . . . Cal Tjader's "Both Sides Of The Coin"
29. Sir John . . . . Blue Mitchell's "Blue's Moods"
30. Sister Sadie . . . . Horace Silver's "Blowin' The Blues Away"
31. Só Danço Samba . . . . "Antonio Carlos Jobim: The Composer Of Desafinado, Plays"; Stan Getz/João Gilberto's "Getz/Gilberto"
32. Song For My Father . . . . Horace Silver's "Song For My Father"
33. Sonnymoon For Two . . . . Sonny Rollins' "A Night At The Village Vanguard"
34. St. James Infirmary . . . . Louis Armstrong's "Satch Blows The Blues"
35. St. Thomas . . . . Sonny Rollins' "Saxophone Colossus"
36. Straight Life . . . . Freddie Hubbard's "Straight Life"
37. Tenor Madness . . . . Sonny Rollins' "Tenor Madness"
38. Trail Dust . . . . Not currently recorded
39. When The Saints Go Marching In . . . . Louis Armstrong's "Golden Greats"
40. Work Song .Cannonball Adderley's "Them Dirty Blues"
41. Yardbird Suite . . . . Charlie Parker's "The Savoy And Dial Master Takes"
42. Z's Blues . . . . Not currently recorded

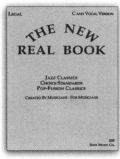

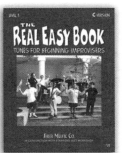

The Real Easy Book Vol. 1
TUNES FOR BEGINNING IMPROVISERS

Published by Sher Music Co. in conjunction with the Stanford Jazz Workshop. $22 list price.

The easiest tunes from Horace Silver, Eddie Harris, Freddie Hubbard, Red Garland, Sonny Rollins, Cedar Walton, Wes Montgomery Cannonball Adderly, etc. Get yourself or your beginning jazz combo sounding good right away with the first fake book ever designed for the beginning improviser. Available in C, Bb, Eb and Bass Clef.

The Real Easy Book Vol. 2
TUNES FOR INTERMEDIATE IMPROVISERS

Published by Sher Music Co. in conjunction with the Stanford Jazz Workshop. Over 240 pages. $29.

The best intermediate-level tunes by: Charlie Parker, John Coltrane, Miles Davis, John Scofield, Sonny Rollins, Horace Silver, Wes Montgomery, Freddie Hubbard, Cal Tjader, Cannonball Adderall, and more! Both volumes feature instructional material tailored for each tune. Perfect for jazz combos! Available in C, Bb, Eb and Bass Clef.

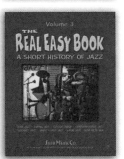

The Real Easy Book Vol. 3
A SHORT HISTORY OF JAZZ

Published by Sher Music Co. in conjunction with the Stanford Jazz Workshop. Over 200 pages. $25.

History text and tunes from all eras and styles of jazz. Perfect for classroom use. Available in C, Bb, Eb and Bass Clef versions.

The Best of Sher Music Co. Real Books
100+ TUNES YOU NEED TO KNOW

A collection of the best-known songs from the world leader in jazz fake books – Sher Music Co.!

Includes songs by: Miles Davis, John Coltrane, Bill Evans, Duke Ellington, Antonio Carlos Jobim, Charlie Parker, John Scofield, Michael Brecker, Weather Report, Horace Silver, Freddie Hubbard, Thelonious Monk, Cannonball Adderley, and many more!

$26. Available in C, Bb, Eb and Bass Clef.

The Serious Jazz Book II
THE HARMONIC APPROACH

By Barry Finnerty, Endorsed by: Joe Lovano, Jamey Aebersold, Hubert Laws, Mark Levine, etc.

- A 200 page, exhaustive study of how to master the harmonic content of songs.
- Contains explanations of every possible type of chord that is used in jazz.
- Clear musical examples to help achieve real harmonic control over melodic improvisation.
- For any instrument. $32. Money back gurantee!

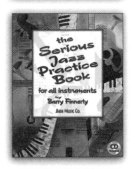

The Serious Jazz Practice Book By Barry Finnerty

A unique and comprehensive plan for mastering the basic building blocks of the jazz language. It takes the most widely-used scales and chords and gives you step-by-step exercises that dissect them into hundreds of cool, useable patterns. Includes CD - $30 list price.

"The book I've been waiting for!" – Randy Brecker.

"The best book of intervallic studies I've ever seen." – **Mark Levine**

The Jazz Theory Book

By Mark Levine, the most comprehensive Jazz Theory book ever published! $38 list price.

- Over 500 pages of text and over 750 musical examples.
- Written in the language of the working jazz musician, this book is easy to read and user-friendly. At the same time, it is the most comprehensive study of jazz harmony and theory ever published.
- Mark Levine has worked with Bobby Hutcherson, Cal Tjader, Joe Henderson, Woody Shaw, and many other jazz greats.

Jazz Piano Masterclass With Mark Levine
"THE DROP 2 BOOK"

The long-awaited book from the author of "The Jazz Piano Book!" A complete study on how to use "drop 2" chord voicings to create jazz piano magic! 68 pages, plus CD of Mark demonstrating each exercise. $19 list.

"Will make you sound like a real jazz piano player in no time." – Jamey Aebersold

Metaphors For The Musician
By Randy Halberstadt

This practical and enlightening book will help any jazz player or vocalist look at music with "new eyes." Designed for any level of player, on any instrument, "Metaphors For The Musician" provides numerous exercises throughout to help the reader turn these concepts into musical reality.

Guaranteed to help you improve your musicianship. 330 pages – $29 list price. Satisfaction guaranteed!

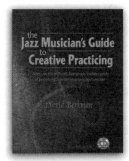

The Jazz Musicians Guide To Creative Practicing
By David Berkman

Finally a book to help musicians use their practice time wisely! Covers tune analysis, breaking hard tunes into easy components, how to swing better, tricks to playing fast bebop lines, and much more! 150+pages, plus CD. $29 list.

"Fun to read and bursting with things to do and ponder." – Bob Mintzer

The 'Real Easy' Ear Training Book
By Roberta Radley

For all musicians, regardless of instrument or experience, this is the most comprehensive book on "hearing the changes" ever published!

- Covers both beginning and intermediate ear training exercises.
- Music Teachers: You will find this book invaluable in teaching ear training to your students.

Book includes 168 pages of instructional text and musical examples, plus two CDs! $29 list price.

The Jazz Singer's Guidebook By David Berkman
A COURSE IN JAZZ HARMONY AND SCAT SINGING FOR THE SERIOUS JAZZ VOCALIST

A clear, step-by-step approach for serious singers who want to improve their grasp of jazz harmony and gain a deeper understanding of music fundamentals.

This book will change how you hear music and make you a better singer, as well as give you the tools to develop your singing in directions you may not have thought possible.

$26 – includes audio CD demonstrating many exercises.

LATIN MUSIC BOOKS, CDs, DVD

The Latin Real Book (C, Bb or Eb)

The only professional-level Latin fake book ever published!
Over 570 pages. Detailed transcriptions exactly as recorded by:

Ray Barretto	Arsenio Rodriguez	Manny Oquendo	Ivan Lins
Eddie Palmieri	Tito Rodriguez	Puerto Rico All-Stars	Djavan
Fania All-Stars	Orquesta Aragon	Issac Delgaldo	Tom Jobim
Tito Puente	Beny Moré	Ft. Apache Band	Toninho Horta
Ruben Blades	Cal Tjader	Dave Valentin	Joao Bosco
Los Van Van	Andy Narell	Paquito D'Rivera	Milton Nascimento
NG La Banda	Mario Bauza	Clare Fischer	Leila Pinheiro
Irakere	Dizzy Gillespie	Chick Corea	Gal Costa
Celia Cruz	Mongo Santamaria	Sergio Mendes	**And Many More!**

The Latin Real Book Sampler CD

12 of the greatest Latin Real Book tunes as played by the original artists: Tito Puente, Ray Barretto, Andy Narell, Puerto Rico Allstars, Bacacoto, etc.

$16 list price. Available in U.S.A. only.

The Conga Drummer's Guidebook By Michael Spiro

Includes CD - $28 list price. The only method book specifically designed for the intermediate to advanced conga drummer. It goes behind the superficial licks and explains how to approach any Afro-Latin rhythm with the right feel, so you can create a groove like the pros!.

"This book is awesome. Michael is completely knowledgable about his subject." – Dave Garibaldi

"A breakthrough book for all students of the conga drum." – Karl Perazzo

Introduction to the Conga Drum - DVD
By Michael Spiro

For beginners, or anyone needing a solid foundation in conga drum technique.

Jorge Alabe – "Mike Spiro is a great conga teacher. People can learn real conga technique from this DVD."

John Santos – "A great musician/teacher who's earned his stripes"

1 hour, 55 minutes running time. $25.

Muy Caliente!

Afro-Cuban Play-Along CD and Book
Rebeca Mauleón - Keyboard
Oscar Stagnaro - Bass
Orestes Vilató - Timbales
Carlos Caro - Bongos
Edgardo Cambon - Congas
Over 70 min. of smokin' Latin grooves!
Stereo separation so you can eliminate the bass or piano. Play-along with a rhythm section featuring some of the top Afro-Cuban musicians in the world! $18.

The True Cuban Bass

By Carlos Del Puerto, (bassist with Irakere) and **Silvio Vergara**, $22.

For acoustic or electric bass; English and Spanish text; Includes CDs of either historic Cuban recordings or Carlos playing each exercise; Many transcriptions of complete bass parts for tunes in different Cuban styles – the roots of Salsa.

101 Montunos
By Rebeca Mauleón

The only comprehensive study of Latin piano playing ever published.

- Bi-lingual text (English/Spanish)
- 2 CDs of the author demonstrating each montuno
- Covers over 100 years of Afro-Cuban styles, including the danzón, guaracha, mambo, merengue and songo—from Peruchin to Eddie Palmieri. $28

The Salsa Guide Book
By Rebeca Mauleón

The only complete method book on salsa ever published! 260 pages. $25.

Carlos Santana – "A true treasure of knowledge and information about Afro-Cuban music."
Mark Levine, author of The Jazz Piano Book. – "This is the book on salsa."
Sonny Bravo, pianist with Tito Puente – "This will be the salsa 'bible' for years to come."
Oscar Hernández, pianist with Rubén Blades – "An excellent and much needed resource."

The Brazilian Guitar Book

By Nelson Faria, one of Brazil's best new guitarists.

- Over 140 pages of comping patterns, transcriptions and chord melodies for samba, bossa, baiaõ, etc.
- Complete chord voicings written out for each example.
- Comes with a CD of Nelson playing each example.
- The most complete Brazilian guitar method ever published! $28.

Joe Diorio – "Nelson Faria's book is a welcome addition to the guitar literature. I'm sure those who work with this volume wiill benefit greatly"

Inside The Brazilian Rhythm Section
By Nelson Faria and Cliff Korman

This is the first book/CD package ever published that provides an opportunity for bassists, guitarists, pianists and drummers to interact and play-along with a master Brazilian rhythm section. Perfect for practicing both accompanying and soloing.

$28 list price for book and 2 CDs - including the charts for the CD tracks and sample parts for each instrument, transcribed from the recording.

The Latin Bass Book
A PRACTICAL GUIDE
By Oscar Stagnaro

The only comprehensive book ever published on how to play bass in authentic Afro-Cuban, Brazilian, Caribbean, Latin Jazz & South American styles. $34.

Over 250 pages of transcriptions of Oscar Stagnaro playing each exercise. Learn from the best!

Includes: 3 Play-Along CDs to accompany each exercise, featuring world-class rhythm sections.

Afro-Caribbean Grooves for Drumset

By Jean-Philippe Fanfant, drummer with Andy narell's band, Sakesho.

Covers grooves from 10 Caribbean nations, arranged for drumset.

Endorsed by Peter Erskine, Horacio Hernandez, etc.

CD includes both audio and video files. $25.

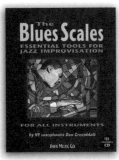